BOOKS BY AUREN URIS

Techniques of Leadership
Action Guide for Job Seekers
Mastery of Management
The Executive Deskbook
Memos for Managers
Executive Housekeeping
The Blue Book of Broadminded Business Behavior
The Executive Interviewer's Deskbook
Executive Dissent—How to Say No and Win

Executive Dissent

How to Say No and Win

Auren Uris

amacom

A Division of
American Management Associations

2-23-95

Library of Congress Cataloging in Publication Data

Uris, Auren.
Executive dissent.

1. Executives. 2. Management. 3. Dissenters.
I. Title.
HF5500.2.U68 658.4 78-9802
ISBN 0-8144-5473-9

Fourth Printing

Credo for the Executive Dissenter

1. I believe it's better to stand up and be counted than to not be worth counting.
2. My organization, right or wrong—but it better be right.
3. If I'm afraid to look my boss in the eye, then I may not want to see myself in the mirror.
4. Working according to my personal principles and values is an important part of my remuneration.
5. An organization impervious to dissent is likely to lack ascent.
6. The right to dissent is as much a part of my job as reading the mail.
7. Protest keeps my head and conscience clear.

Preface

THIS book differs from others on the subject of dissent in organizations in two major respects: previous treatments have been in general, abstract terms, while this is seen as a practical discussion; and the focus here is on dissent by executives—the executive versus the organization. The aim is to show how dissent can enrich both executives and organizations.

Dissent can be a tremendous force for change. When it originates at the higher corporate levels, it becomes, for the organization, a constructive form of self-questioning and redirection. Equally important are the implications of dissent in terms of the effectiveness and career objectives of the executive. The executive who knows how to register dissent becomes:

- More his or her own person.
- Alert to the possibility of improving the status quo.

- A constant source of feedback for the organization as a whole.

The executive who knows how to deal with the dissent of others can

- Strengthen organizational policy and decision making.
- Use the dissent to sharpen his or her own thinking.
- Improve the process of dissent so that maximum benefits may be derived, both individually and organizationally, while destructive aspects are minimized.

When misunderstood or ignored, dissent can handicap growth, day-to-day operations, and the self-fulfillment of individual executives. Fortunately, the process of dissent has been stimulated by several recent trends. First, a rising of expectations in the general population has tended to favor a turning to personal values and a search for self-fulfillment, both of which encourage executives to assert their personal views. And the current entrance of more and more women into management circles has increased the likelihood of dissent. It's not a question of militancy, but rather that a woman's fresher view of principle and fairness often sparks questions and protests. If their protests are handled constructively, management may reap much benefit from this source of nonconformist opinion.

The new wave of open-mindedness definitely strengthens individuals in relation to their organization, and the aware executive should learn how to make the most of it. Thus, this book's major aim: to foster intelligent dissent among executives and to suggest better ways to deal with it.

In studying executive dissent, one can uncover principles around which an organization is built, and also reveal much about individual executives' own values. And in looking closely at the process of dissent, one may come to some new and important appraisals of organizational realities and to a new picture of one's own submerged self.

Acknowledgments

Gratitude to the many colleagues, friends, and professionals willing to share their views and experience has been expressed by me on an individual basis. In addition, public appreciation is due those whose help has been extensive and continuing. This group includes:

Colleagues at the Research Institute of America: Jane Bensahel, Ruth Burger, Joseph Cowley, Raymond Concannon, Ken Dobrer, Patricia Durston, Mary Jollon, Domenica Mortati, Marjorie Noppel, Tom Quick, Trevor Thomas, Louise Trenta, and Barbara Whitmore.

For library services and general assistance in running down study and survey sources: Inese Rudzitis and Joy Elbaum, of the Research Institute Library.

For outstanding help with the physical preparation of the manuscript: Winifred Mathie, Doris

Horvath, Lesley Lull, Lisa Golden, Louise Ligato, Ellen Taylor, and Fay Rossi.

Suzanne Sage, for enlightening views on aspects of behavior that represent important breaks with the past.

Doris Reichbart, for helpful discussions on some of the day-to-day manifestations of dissent, and specific case histories.

And finally, the executives at Sweetheart Plastics of Wilmington, Massachusetts, especially Samuel Shapiro, George Shumrak, and Dick Tufenkjian, for their stimulating views and conversation on organizational dissent; and Betsy Howe of that same organization, for communications and facilitating assistance.

Auren Uris

Contents

Part III Making Dissent Constructive

PART I

Setting the Stage

Protest is an organizational process. As such it has structure and a series of elements that tend to follow each other in sequence. In addition to its mechanistic aspects, protest often becomes a highly personal and emotional act. Executives who take issue with their organization may be playing for huge stakes, not only for themselves, but also for the organization. It is basic to the concept of this book that protest is healthy and stimulating. The trouble is, even in organizations that agree with this view, the connotations of dissent—the skepticism with which it is often perceived—may prevent those organizations from deriving any benefit from it.

The six chapters comprising Part I deal with the eruption of executive dissent—the forces that create it, and the painful consequences that may follow if it is bottled up, prevented from following its natural and productive course.

CHAPTER 1

When an Executive Begs to Differ

PAUL STARR wakes up one morning feeling terrible. "Hangover," is his first thought. But then he remembers. His unhappy state has nothing to do with alcohol; he has been going through some bad days and sleepless nights, and this is the morning he is finally going to meet with his boss. The time has come to say his piece. "Roger, I've been thinking over your decision about the Green Hills subdivision," Paul intends to say. "If we go ahead on the basis you propose, I feel it will be a violation of everything this company stands for. Customers will never be able to realize anything on their investment; it will be bad for the surrounding community . . . and I'm not even touching on the question of legality. So, either this project gets shelved, or I resign."

You Disagree Because You Must— The Dissenter's Imperative

People may differ with their bosses or with company policy, and usually the disagreement is easily settled. But there are situations when in differing with an organization policy or decision, a major rift develops. The headache Paul Starr felt is typical of the upsets that may result. And everyone in the organization—even the firm itself—may suffer to one degree or another.

Since the executive–versus–organization conflict may cause damage, the ideal solution might seem to be that of minimizing the situation, to counsel evasion tactics that will cool things off for all concerned. But it is an oversimplification to think that dissent, like indigestion, can be eliminated by some mollifying medicine. Furthermore, such palliatives are not even desirable, as we will soon see.

True, minor protest can be overlooked with little consequence, or even considered as part of the regular give and take of the working day. But more to the point, the *benefits* of dissent are of such overriding importance that even considering an under-the-rug treatment should be unacceptable to any management interested in vitality and growth. As for the dissenter, he or she has, at the very least, an emotional stake in being heard. And though the matter may be trivial, the organization's and other people's future may still be affected.

When You Challenge the Front Office

In a typical conflict, the organization's view is attacked as being inferior to that of the executive dissenter. Once the dissent becomes a voiced protest, there must be an organization response. In some situations dissent *can* be throttled. In specific instances, it *has* been—in nations as well as in corporations—but only for relatively short periods of time. Generally, we seldom have the choice of approving or eliminating dissent. It seems to be as much a phenomenon of organizations as communication itself. One authoritative source reports:

> The military services, the Catholic Church, labor unions, professional athletics, and federal civil service—all have provided examples of dissent and even revolt. In such a climate, it would be foolhardy to cling to the hope that the corporation is immune.*

Conflict is indeed a constant fact of business life. Managers know it firsthand. Industrial psychologists study it continually. Managerial experts spend considerable time analyzing its roots and seeking ways of minimizing the consequences. But really, one would think that the sheer prevalence of conflict between individual and organization suggests that it is inherent in the system and cannot be eliminated either by whim or will.

Accordingly, this book aims not to suggest ways and means of eliminating conflict but rather to propose concepts, attitudes, and procedures that can make it a vitalizing element.

Further, it is intended to put dissent into perspective by describing in detail the misconceptions and errors made by both executives and organiza-

* "Responding to the Employee Voice," Dan H. Fenn, Jr. and Daniel Yankelovich, *Harvard Business Review*, May–June 1972.

tions in dealing with it. While many organizations large and small have a constructive approach perfectly capable of utilizing the benefits of dissent, these too may find the concepts and recommendations advanced helpful in evaluating and improving present practices. To present its points, the assumption is made that organizations view dissent and protest dimly. While it is understood that some companies do otherwise, the fact that the large majority misconstrues the benefits of dissent emphasizes that the device is not farfetched and therefore does not do violence to the basic realities.

Dissent as an Organizational Asset

Observers of the management scene have recently clarified the role of the nonconformist individual in organizations.* More and more, the individuals who take issue with the traditional views are seen in a favorable light. Such an attitude flourishes when the temper of the times provides more individuals willing to see the organization with something less than reverence, who receive edicts from the top as something less than laws carved in stone, and who want to inject personal values into their workaday responsibilities.

The growing acceptance of these views has extensive implications for businesses and the people who run them. If indeed dissent is desirable in management affairs, then it behooves managers to learn how to recognize, propagate, and use it. And, if em-

* Thomas Rotondi, Jr., "The Innovator and the Ritualist: A Study in Conflict," *Personnel Journal*, June 1974.

ployees are beginning to differ more frequently on questions of operations and policy, then it becomes necessary for managers to learn how to make that dissent useful to themselves and the organization.

The Blinding Glare of Self-Satisfaction

Self-satisfaction becomes an obstacle to dissent even when—perhaps one should say *especially* when—it is based on organizational success. In companies in which "business is good," or in which outstanding success has persisted over a long period of time, the entire organization may be pervaded by strong feelings of self-approval.

The attitude one is likely to encounter in such a company is that "management knows best, and the bottom line proves it." If might indeed makes right, and those in authority are omniscient, then there would be no place for dissent on the work scene. But that kind of organizational super-wisdom is a pipe dream. Management often does not know best. What happens in the absence of a questioning voice is that decisions and plans get implemented without the benefit of choosing among alternatives. And ideas that originate from traditional and parochial sources tend to be repetitive, uninspiring, and obsolete.

Naked Emperors and Fully Clothed Fools

Similar in some ways to the self-satisfaction based on superior performance—however temporary—is a smugness based on self-delusion. Perhaps because of a company's high standing in its field—"We're Number One," as the advertisements claim—people at the top may feel they can do no wrong. They see themselves as being omnipotent. Their every glance in the mirror reveals a beautiful image. And so in these executive suites one finds the Emperor's Clothes Syndrome: the emperor, reinforced by the sycophancy of his followers, believes that he is beautifully attired when indeed he is naked; and without the challenge of a clear-eyed dissenter, he runs the risk of sooner or later appearing a fool.

The Dilemma Posed by Dissent

Conflict in the business world, despite the attention it gets from so many quarters, continues to be hazily understood. People for whom it is a day-to-day preoccupation—for example, business managers—often find themselves puzzled by a dilemma: on the one hand, the managerial theoreticians arguing that dissent is desirable, and on the other hand the more conventional view that harmony is the greater good. And some managers see protest as recalcitrance, an ego trip, and certainly not businesslike.

And there is the personal threat to managers confronted by a dissenter. Their authority, or judgment, seems to be under attack. Perhaps company policy mandates toleration, even encouragement, of the employee who is finding fault with one or another policy or procedure. But psychological defenses become mobilized through a logic of their own, and it is difficult to put aside feelings of hostility or rejection.

The very concept of "businesslike" suggests orderliness. Protest is thus seen as interference, boat-rocking, an irresponsible attempt to block progress, proof of a lack of sympathy with organization goals.

Dissent and Organization Renewal

But as the nature of dissent and its consequences comes into focus, one sees not only that it has a place in organizational life, but that it can be put to constructive use. The stakes may be high: it could mean one or more employees' livelihood; it could jeopardize the "muscle tone" of the organization (the mechanisms for responsive movement); and ultimately, it can involve the fate of the enterprise itself. Nevertheless, people with a great deal of managerial experience strongly support its effectiveness as a growth factor.

> Conflict releases energy at every level of human affairs—energy that can produce positive, constructive results. Two things should be recognized here. First, that such conflict is an absolutely predictable social phenomenon. Second, that conflict should not be repressed, but channeled to useful purposes. Both of these realities lie at the heart of organization renewal.*

* Adapted from Gordon L. Lippitt, *Organization Renewal,* New York, Appleton-Century-Crofts, 1969.

What lies behind that promising phrase, "organization renewal"? Specifically, what are the potential gains and losses of dissent?

Damage versus Benefits

If dissent were without risk, and if it were a consistently benign process, it would flourish. However, since this is not the case, there is always the potential for both good and bad results.

Warren H. Schmidt, senior lecturer in behavioral science at the UCLA Graduate School of Management, has spelled out some of the possible consequences of organizational disagreement*:

Potential Benefits	*Potential Damage*
Better ideas are produced.	Some people feel defeated and demeaned.
People are forced to question their assumptions and search for new approaches.	Distance between people is increased.
Long-standing problems surface and are dealt with.	A climate of distrust and suspicion develops.
People are forced to clarify their views.	People and departments that need to cooperate look only after their own narrow interests. Resistance—active or passive—develops where teamwork is needed. Some people leave because of the turmoil.
The tension stimulates interest and creativity.	
People have a chance to test their capabilities.	

One advantage of Schmidt's analysis is that it makes it easier to pinpoint the benefits of conflict

* "Conflict," *Management Review*, December 1974.

one wants and the harm to be avoided. To gain the benefits and avoid the pitfalls, one must take a close look at the insights, information, and ideas of those who are responsible for dealing with dissent and protest.

Why It's Tough to Be a Boat Rocker

Business has its stereotypes, and one of the better known is that of the boat rocker, the individual capable of viewing even the most revered golden calf of management with a jaundiced eye. Obviously, this fellow is hardly a hallowed figure in the pantheon of management stereotypes. The term rocking the boat is usually used in the pejorative sense, and is equated with nuisance and troublemaking. The main reason for the bad reputation is that too many managers have failed to notice the constructive criticism that often underlies these peoples' protests.

As Warren Schmidt has pointed out, the organizations that question their own assumptions and subject their ideas and plans to criticism are those that are able to come up with the fresh approaches and breakthroughs that make for profitable innovation. Let's look at the barriers that stand in the way of accepting dissent. For one thing, many managers lack the self-confidence it takes to subject their thinking to the criticism of others. Protest from a dissenting colleague can be threatening. Of course there are executives who are willing to take ideas to their staff or colleagues and say, "Here it is. What's wrong with it?" Much more common, however, are those executives who present a favored idea with the intention of having it admired. And that raises the question, If an idea is truly a good one, why would anyone hesitate to put it on the block for inspection?

The answer seems to be that the ego craves the more immediate satisfaction of having one's thinking accepted and applauded without having to endure a critique. The fact is that we all have uncertainties and anxieties, and these are likely to be triggered by criticism or—as criticism is often perceived—by attack by other people. It is understandable, then, that a person who rocks the boat is seldom a welcome figure in the business world.

A complex mechanism has developed to stifle, perhaps obliquely, the person who dissents. One of the most crushing things that can be said about a manager is that he or she is being "negative." This label is especially unfair because it suggests the opposite of what was really intended. And the truth is, constructive criticism can be one of the strongest contributions an individual can make in the generation and refinement of ideas in business.

For both the individual executive and the organization as a whole, any pitfalls placed in the way of dissent should be eliminated wherever possible. To not do so may mean losing the benefits of dissent, as well as the services of the dissenter. For these days, with our increased expectations of the job environment, creative employees are less likely to stay in situations where they are continually thwarted.

Additional Fruits of Dissent

We know that, optimally, organizations change, develop, grow. A good deal of top management thought is given to the problem of assuring the vitality of the organization. For example, this interest is reflected in the attention given by Personnel to phasing out less capable staff—who may range from people who should not have been hired in the first place, to those who become obsolete as a result of the increased sophistication of the organization's activities, and to those whose dwindling performance suggests replacement by new blood.

A key factor in maintaining the dynamism of an organization involves its handling of dissent and protest. Whereas there is no doubt that ideas improve when subjected to criticism and contrary opinion, the problem is that dissent is not limited to disagreeing on small matters. It is when big problems emerge—and still the company encourages criticism—that the difference between a self-satisfied, yet moribund, organization, and one committed to growth, emerges. Any company that fosters dissent at the management level will at least gain the following:

Self-awareness. Management acquires greater insight into what it is doing. Faced with the possibility of being second-guessed by others, managers will give broader and deeper consideration to key issues.

Ongoing critique. In organizations where dissent is constructively channeled, it can become a way of discerning shifts in values—in themselves harbingers of change. These values may concern everything from employees' dress to the need for managerial autonomy.

In the course of its routine operations, every organization makes many decisions, takes many actions, develops certain basic policies. Since organizations, like individuals, are fallible, it is not surprising that somewhere along the line an executive is going to find fault. Whether this is an advantage or disadvantage may depend upon the executive's perspective and motive. It's an advantage when the executive can view the organization policy afresh and see it for what it is *supposed* to be and what it is *likely* to accomplish. In fact, this person may well know something that the people who have developed the policy don't. On the other hand, the executive may be at a disadvantage if he or she has not been involved in the formative process that led to the policy in question. In other words, the criticism, though well-intended, is irrelevant because it hasn't considered all the pertinent facts.

So, when it comes to dissent, think before you leap. Know where you're jumping from and where you expect to land. And check these same points in those who voice their opposition when you are in the role of organization representative.

There are unmatchable benefits to the process of dissent. But in order for them to accrue to both organization and executive dissenter, a realistic awareness of what is involved, and how to deal with it, is essential. The next chapter describes that major element in the process of dissent—the dissenter.

CHAPTER 2

What Makes an Executive Say, "I've Had It!"

I'm a good company man, I've been a good company man all my life; but damn it, there are times when you just should stand up on your feet and protest!*

WHAT "times" make a previously assenting manager switch to the role of dissident? What situations might cause executives to take exception to the organization view?

* "Responding to the Employee Voice," Dan H. Fenn, Jr. and Daniel Yankelovich, *Harvard Business Review,* May–June 1972.

Areas of Dissent

Usually, executives must blend together personal and organizational attitudes and values. What is good for the company is seen as good for the manager. But situations may develop in which an individual and the organization no longer see eye to eye. Pinpointing these situations helps clarify a crucial part of the dissent process. Here are some of the grounds on which an executive and the organization may differ:

Operating decisions. For example, an executive takes issue with a decision to start a low-price line, or vigorously opposes modifying a standard product for a specialized market.

Personnel practices. Things such as mandatory retirement at a specific age or a new plan for a pension fund can spark sharp disagreement. A manager might protest strongly at what he thinks are ill-considered arrangements.

Organization affiliations. The company itself or top executives are affiliated, for instance, with clubs that discriminate against minorities. Minority employees or sympathizers might demand an end to such memberships.

Safety. An engineer in a nuclear training facility refuses to start up a reactor despite a direct order. He sees a real safety hazard there, regardless of management's contrary opinion.

Unethical practices. Key people in the organization are known for, or suspected of, shady financial dealings, yet management seems uncaring. An ethical executive might not want the organization to tolerate illegality or corruption and voices vigorous protest.

Outer Limits

The list, of course, could be enlarged. Not entirely germane to this book, but extremely common nonetheless, are actions of the following variety:

Grievances. Every organization entertains a number of complaints centering on the many things that people, fairly or unjustly, find fault with on the work scene. The objections might concern an office carpet retained so long that its color has faded, or the temperature at which the thermostat is set. These matters, though important to the people involved, are routine problems usually resolved by discussion.

Whistle-blowing. Individuals protest what they consider improper behavior on the part of other employees in the belief that the public interest overrides the interest of the organization. Such behavior may involve corruption, violence, fraud, or some other socially harmful activity which, though it may be or vital concern to the public, is not within the scope of this book.

It is useful to describe a certain character who, by the nature of his protests, is also not relevant to this book. He is the Perennial Rebel, the individual with a propensity for causing trouble. To him, protest is something to undertake for its own sake. The emotional satisfaction in kicking over the traces, raising the roof, rocking the boat, and so on is incentive enough. These people like the feeling of combat, of not conforming to the accepted order of things.

This is not to say that there aren't justifications for their conduct. But unlike other kinds of people who dissent, the natural rebel is on an ego trip in which ordinary considerations of the business scene are incidental. The rebel can be easily identified by the frequency of protests, their vehemence, and their irrelevance. Once the habitual nature of the rebel's protest is noticed, when its inappropriateness becomes obvious, the usual treatment for misfits may be applied to minimize interference with organizational affairs. Few companies can tolerate the destructive nuisance of the self-indulgent rebel. In routine business practice, this individual must be stopped or else eliminated for the good of the company and the peace of mind of the other employees.

The Feelings That Lead to Protest

Having identified some of the issues that often become the subject of dissent, the next step is to examine the *why* of the process. Why do dissenters separate themselves from the crowd and in so doing not only risk becoming isolated within the firm, but now have to work extra hard to substantiate their case?

The dissenter who speaks up may have only mild disagreement with the status quo, or could have a raging anger. Probably a typical mood is that portrayed by the manager at the beginning of this chapter. He is angry. He suggests that the provocation is becoming sufficiently strong for him to take action. But what is the provocation about? Surprisingly, in studying numerous instances of organizational protest, one finds that only a few factors account for virtually all of the many possible complaints.

Some people see the act of protest as a sort of transcendence of the normal limits of behavior. Perhaps it is an exaggeration to frame protest on the work scene as though it were no different from a struggle to change the fate of nations. The great dissidents of history, such as the leaders of the American Revolution, seem a far cry from the executive who complains about some limitation of the company dining room. But it is equally wrong to view executive protest merely as evidence of personality quirks. It is precisely because protest *does* represent something unique in executive behavior that it deserves special attention.

In looking further into the kinds of situations that lead an executive to voice protest, one should search for the elements in a conflict that play on the sensitivities of an individual and thus create a need for self-assertion. Let's give the anonymous manager who began this chapter with, ". . . there are times when you should protest!" a name, and put him in a situation that would bring him to his feet in strong disagreement.

Frank Lloyd, employed with the same organization for 20 years, has never felt the need to protest a company act or decision. But one day he's in his boss's office, livid and shaking. "B.J., I just saw Paul Hutter and although he didn't come right out and say so, he made some pretty broad hints that I was expected to retire on my next birthday. I want you to know I feel good enough for another ten years, and I want your assurance. . . ."

In short, Lloyd wants no part of management's decision to have him retire before he is ready to do so. Leaving aside the pros and cons of the retirement issue, it is still possible to pinpoint the reasons why Lloyd, with never a protest in his record, would speak up now. First, there is *personal involvement.* The situation touches him in a deeply personal way. Second, there is the likelihood of *loss.* The threat may be financial and/or psychological, arousing fears of a change in his life that he was not yet ready to accept. And third, implicit in the protest is anger at an *injustice.* Put into words, it would come out something like this: "After years of my loyalty, the company can't be so unfair as to give me the heave-ho." In other instances of protest, these three elements may be modified considerably. Let's take them one at a time:

Personal involvement. In Frank Lloyd's case, the suggestion of retirement and its consequences were directed at him personally. But executives may feel involved for less direct reasons. For instance, one executive reacted strongly against a new rule that discontinued a practice by which employees could purchase company products at a discount. The executive had little personal interest in these purchases—in fact, he never made any—but felt that its PR value was worth the inconvenience and costs it incurred. In this case it was the executive's identification with the company and its well-being that spurred him to voice dissent.

Loss. This factor can become attenuated and subtle, and yet be crucial. In the example above, where the company wants to end a tradition, you might consciously miss the old ways. Or a sense of loss could arise in your identifying with other employees who would feel deprived upon losing a privilege. In other cases, the sense of loss might lie in having a cherished principle subverted or contradicted. An executive who believes in participatory management might resent—and protest—an arbitrary and seemingly unwise directive to employees, about which they have not been consulted.

Injustice. An executive whom we shall call Dave Slade has asked for an audience with the president of his company. He begins the conversation as follows: "Mr. Gorvin, when I took this job I knew it was with a family-owned company, but in talking with Al Perry in Personnel at the time, I was assured that management was not going to load all of the desirable spots in the organization with family members. Al said something like, 'We're aware of the need to keep the spirit of competition and incentive alive.'

"As you know, I've been sales manager for six years now, and I think you'll agree that I've been doing one hell of a job. But I've heard that there is a plan to restructure Sales, and that there is now going to be a vice president of Marketing. Well, I believe I'm the logical and best-qualified person for that spot, but there are rumors going around to the effect that your son is going to get the position.

"I don't think I'm naive. And I'm up on all the rules of management that say blood is thicker than water. But I don't consider myself water. Without criticizing your son Eric's capabilities—I think he's done a good job as a salesman—I don't believe there is any doubt that the V.P. spot should be mine."

Just how effective Slade's protest will be can't be predicted; the example is intended only to illustrate how resentment of organizational unfairness or injustice leads to protest. Also included under this heading of unfairness are such matters as bias, real or fancied, of an executive against a subordinate; favoritism in general; and the old sure-fire way to stimulate protest, a new policy that deprives employees of a previously enjoyed privilege.

Matters of Principle

Aside from personal issues are those that have to do with inner convictions and that may or may not involve personal loss or gain. Some of the more common issues:

Questionable values. Company policies and decisions may reflect basic values which may precipitate protest. The conflict below derives from the expectation on the part of management that an individual should make personal sacrifices for the good of the organization.

Sales manager Tom Pace is called into the office of his boss, the vice president of marketing. "Tom," the V.P. says, "we've finally firmed up our plans on redistributing territories. It's been decided that your particular capability in developing territories will do us the most good in the southeast region. We'll be ready to open our regional headquarters there in three months and we'd like you to take over."

Though the offer is meant to be a promotion, Pace does not see it that way. He says, "But, Larry, making the change would be extremely difficult for me right now. We're very much involved in our community. The kids love their schools. It would mean a major disruption."

"I'm sorry to hear that," his boss says, "but I'm afraid that's the way it's got to be."

"In that case," replies Pace, "you've got a decision to make. You either take me off the spot, or you lose me."

Pace makes his protest in the starkest terms possible. Management must now review the situation, and reexamine the values implicit in its stand that an employee must put the company's needs above his own.

Questionable judgments. Some decisions or acts of management are not rooted in a value or attitude, but simply reflect an opinion on the effectiveness of a particular course of action. This too can lead to protest. For example, Joan Riordan is head of research and development for a drug manufacturer. She gets a memo from the front office detailing the marketing schedule of a new headache remedy. She is upset by the announcement, and arranges a meeting with her boss, the executive vice president.

"Jim," she says, "I thought we had agreed not to go on the market until we had finished another round of testing. You know I wasn't satisfied with the first results."

"But, Joan, you have to admit that the findings were favorable, definitely within limits that justify our going public."

"If you must know, I think there's been considerable polishing of those figures. I think people around here have gotten so fired up with the idea of getting this on the market before the competition does, that they've looked the other way when anything negative came along."

"Are you saying the reports have been falsified?"

"I'm saying that in my professional opinion we're taking a terrible chance with the future of the company if we put that product out without more stringent checking."

Protests like Riordan's are comparatively common. People at all levels and types of jobs are in a position to have opinions about management decisions. And when they are sufficiently involved in their work, when there is a strong professional or personal identification with company operations, this type of protest will be made. Dissent of this nature is an example of the way management can monitor the feelings of employees who care.

The organization versus society. The final category of protest is one in which an employee takes it upon himself to defend the public against what is seen as an antisocial act. In practice, this is a special kind of "questionable value." But it is treated separately because it represents an increasing source of protest, and involves public as well as private good.

Paul Tyler is a department manager for an organization that produces a spray-can product. At the present time there is considerable scientific opinion to the effect that fluorocarbon gases used in spray cans are slowly destroying the earth's ozone layer and threaten to affect the climate and thus the well-being of all creatures. On his way to work Tyler reads an item in the newspaper describing an experiment that reinforces the ozone studies. He is disturbed because his division is producing a product that is adding to the very thing that the scientists claim is dangerous.

What should Paul Tyler do? Should he place immediate company interest above that of the public at large? Or should he attempt a protest that, though it may upset management, will force it to reconsider its position? This kind of controversy and dissent is becoming increasingly important as more individuals and firms acquire an environmental awareness.

The Five Choices

In Tyler's case—and for protesters in general—there are five possible resolutions:

1. *Agreement.* Tyler might get his company to go along with his views. Accordingly, there would be an attempt to redesign the product so as to eliminate the chances of environmental damage.
2. *Modification.* The organization might be persuaded to make some changes, but practical considerations prevent complete concurrence. In this case, management would seek to minimize the possible undesirable consequences.
3. *Turndown.* The dissenter makes his pitch, but it is no dice. The higher levels don't buy his arguments or viewpoint. The failure may leave the protester disappointed, disgruntled. Some face may have been lost, and a sense of failure may linger for a while. But he has *not* laid his job on the line—the course taken in the approach below.
4. *Resignation.* Tyler might have to go to his boss and explain that he feels duty-bound to quit a job that is socially destructive. This move, representing a high level of ethics, has

the obvious drawback of leaving Tyler unemployed—a hardship even if only temporary, and especially so for an individual with family responsibilities.

5. *Acceptance of the status quo.* No dissent is made. Tyler can continue to work and go about his job in his usual manner. Most likely, however, if he is at all a sensitive individual, he will have acquired a double-edged burden of guilt. First, he'll feel he's doing something wrong—that is, socially harmful—and second, he no longer sees himself as an employee in good standing, but one who is at odds with the organization—a lonely and uncertain role.

In considering whether to make a protest, the executive can use these possible consequences to weigh the possible good against the expected bad. Then, knowing what could go wrong or right, the executive can plan a suitable action.

CHAPTER 3

The Confrontation—Shoot-out in the Executive Suite

YOU'VE witnessed the scene a dozen times if you're any kind of movie fan at all. After a considerable amount of story has unwound—cattle have been rustled, squatters have been shot at, all kinds of derring-do has taken place in dance halls and saloons—finally comes the climactic scene. The two gunfighters face each other from opposite ends of a dusty street. Slowly they approach each other, tension obvious in every move and muscle.

The typical Western gunfight is not unlike the showdown between a dissenter and an executive who does not yet view protest as a beneficial process. There is the same ominous quiet while the two individuals, for all intents and purposes adversaries to the death, approach one another, trigger fingers itching, while an appalled and excited audience watches from behind curtained windows.

Of course, this shouldn't—and needn't—happen. For when enlightenment and open-mindedness are part of an organization's climate, the win–lose atmosphere disappears and a desirable receptivity to dissent can be expected. And, as in the Western, the two sworn foes can be reconciled, not by the love of a good woman, but by a mutual awareness of the validity and value of dissent as an organizational process.

From Disagreement to Protest

An executive differs—that is, disagrees—with management on some specific matter. The logical next step is that of protest.

Protest, formal or informal, is the crucial element in organizational confrontation, an act that interrupts the ordinary flow of events and brings into being—somewhat like an island rising out of the sea—a new configuration on the work scene. Before the protest, there is usually a state of harmony, where everyone either agrees with management or at least is willing to go along with it. Afterwards, however, that spirit of concord has been disturbed by a protesting voice. The raising of an issue breaks up the monolith of unity into confronting parties: the protester against the organization representative.

The protest phase highlights the three basic elements that come into being during the confrontation. An understanding of these components will assist later in optimizing prescriptions for handling dissent. The act of protest transforms a placid unity into three distinct elements. These are as follows.

The Protester—the executive who for one reason or another has come to feel strongly enough about something to step forward and make clear his disagreement. This individual need not necessarily go it alone; well-wishers, adherents, and allies may join in. If so, the confrontation often takes on a more serious aspect, since the possible consequences may be compounded as a result of the larger number of people involved.

The Issue—the principle, policy, or action over which the protester and management have locked horns. In reality not all protests are defensible, and some may be totally unjustified. Nonetheless, management must deal with these as well as those that are potentially constructive.

The Listener—a person with some degree of authority who by his position or personality is a natural choice to give the protester a hearing. Clearly the listener is crucial in determining whether the protest becomes destructive or constructive.

The Values Collision

The dissenter usually faces the organization's representative in a basic conflict over values: his against the organization's. If the organization views dissent as a threat rather than a potential benefit, the conflict is seen only as a win–lose situation. If the dissenter loses, the organization wins. If the dissenter wins, the organization—certainly its image of infallibility—suffers a setback. The win–lose aspect of the confrontation is intensified by rigid attitudes on the part of either the dissenter or the executive who has to hear him out. The former has objectives that militate against the organization's position, while the latter sees the protester as an adversary who must be fought.

When the Organization Representative Must Decide

The dissenter, as pointed out in the previous chapter, can expect five possible outcomes: agreement, modification, turndown, resignation, or acceptance of the organization's view. But different objectives loom for the listening executive. They line up in more or less the following order.

Eliminate the protest. Where dissent is seen as an undesirable interference or interruption, the logical goal for the listener is to try to quiet the protest so that the organization's view prevails.

Minimum concession. In many confrontations the company representative will decide that the way to minimize potential damage is to, in a sense, buy off the protest by accepting certain aspects of the protester's view and incorporating them into the policy or decision. This tack, essentially a compromise, may be both practical and wise, for it may be an effort not so much to dodge the dissenter, but to accept worthwhile elements in his criticism.

Reprisal. In organizations where protest is viewed as treason, there may be an attempt to punish the protester, in extreme cases by firing him. Of course, in the enlightened organization, confrontation between a dissenter and a mediating executive is not viewed as a shoot-out but rather an opportunity for improvement—a comparison of the values represented by the organization and the protester, and a process of examination and evaluation that could result in a vital hybrid incorporating the virtues of both parties.

The Five Nerve Tauteners

In unenlightened settings, the negative aspects of dissent are amplified by certain tension-inducing factors, which might be called *nerve tauteners:*

1. *Others are watching.* Few protests are made of which other employees remain ignorant. For the organization an increase in the number of involved people increases apprehension. Organizational strife can (and sometimes does) get out of hand. The larger the number of adversaries, the more serious the threat.
2. *Organization on trial.* For the inflexible organization, any challenge to its authority threatens to reveal a weakness. Its management views the organization as though it were sacred, incapable of doing wrong. Dissent puts this somewhat unrealistic view to the test.
3. *Emotions.* Emotionality on the work scene is almost always unwanted and upsetting. Whether it's a secretary in tears or an executive raging over a fancied personal injustice, management by and large does not like employees importing emotions into the job envi-

ronment. They should confine them to the home, so the attitude goes. But by its nature, dissent tends to encourage people to pull out the emotional stops, particularly when the original impetus for protest is an emotional reaction of some kind. This possibility further amplifies executive tension.

4. *Personal stakes.* For executives on either side of the table, the confrontation is fraught with possible damaging results. Reputations may be injured. The dissenter may fall from grace and be labeled a rebel. The listening executive must also worry about how he will look as a result of what transpires during the confrontation and of any judgments rendered.
5. *Consequences for the organization.* Most confrontations involving protest have built-in limits in terms of how large a scale the protest may be. It takes a particularly crucial matter to have visible impact on an organization—as in the hiring or firing of a top executive. Nevertheless, even when the dissent involves a minor matter, the outcome can still affect the climate and reputation of the organization. For example, repressive judgments tend to reinforce the image of an insensitive, rigid, or authoritarian company. On the other hand, an organization that is overly quick to give in to protest might be seen as weak.

It's up to both the dissenter and the listening executive to meet in such a way as to minimize the shoot-out nature of the hearing. Each individual can help maximize the benefits of a confrontation and cancel out negative factors. Furthermore, they can do this without deferring to one another or watering down their respective roles.

What the Dissenter Can Do

As the person making the protest, you as much as anyone are in a position to create a constructive atmosphere in the meeting. Here are some ways you can do this:

Go easy on the recruiting. A must-win strategy might suggest that you prepare for the confrontation by lining up as much support as you can. This may be a perfectly realistic move. As a matter of fact, your decision to protest or not may even be based on how many colleagues you can get to back you. But keep in mind the old military maxim: once a powerful weapon is mobilized it becomes difficult not to use it. In other words, drumming up the support of like-minded people may actually put you in a bind by forcing you to adopt a position too far from your original stance.

Watch the timing. The factor of timing is important in the sense that, as the person initiating the protest, you have the opportunity of scheduling it for maximum effect. The timing factor also relates to the point at issue. It is up to the dissenter to calculate when the protest can be made most logically and effectively.

Alice Fleet, for example, was considerably upset by a decision made by her division head to cancel a series of meetings that she had come to depend on for contact with executives up the line. There were to be two more meetings before the new schedule was followed. She wisely refrained from rushing right in to make a protest to her boss. Instead she waited until the next meeting, during which she made careful notes of the real benefits she got out of the discussions—the information disseminated, agreements made between department leaders, ideas developed, and so on. Then, right after the meeting she asked her boss for an interview at which she presented an argument that was backed by evidence and was to the point. Had she moved right after the announcement, her argument could have been dismissed as being not carefully thought out. If she had waited until *after* the new system had started, it might have been too late; her boss might have felt that the new arrangement could not be reversed.

Circumstances will vary with each case. The important thing is that you strike the best possible balance between a protest made prematurely and one made belatedly.

Don't bury your emotions. It may not always be possible to be friendly. The fact is that from time to time protest will include an element of outrage which cannot and should not be glossed over. Robotizing interpersonal exchanges is neither desirable nor effective. However, no matter how justified an extreme emotion may be it's incumbent upon the dissenter to make emotionality an undercurrent of the discussion, rather than its main content. Remember, in most cases you know the executive with whom you are lodging your dissent, and you may have a history of warm and friendly contact with this individual. Why put it aside now when it can really facilitate the business at hand?

Be specific. If a protest is to be effective it must aim for a specific judgment. In your role of dissident you have to decide what kind of response you really want and when you would like to have it. Somewhere before the meeting ends you must let the listening executive know what your expectations are. For example: "I think, Mr. Smith, that a week ought to be enough time for you to look into the facts I've brought up and to talk to some of the other people. Will you give me an answer by next Friday?" Be prepared, however, to have your view modified by the other person. Generally there's no reason not to accept something like, "A week doesn't give me enough time. I'll need two weeks."

Finally, in order to leave the interview feeling satisfied, you must do what you can to ensure that there has been a meeting of the minds—despite some disagreement—and that a decision on the protest will be forthcoming.

What the Listener Can Do

There are specific moves the organization's representative can make to clear the decks for a constructive meeting. In general, as the listener or mediator, you should be guided by the same attitudes and principles that are helpful in dealing with any employee or colleague: friendliness, open-mindedness, courtesy. But because of the special nature of this confrontation, you may want to show even more flexibility. Following are a few ideas that can facilitate purposeful discussion.

Emphasize your willingness to listen. Even if the protest catches you by surprise, try as quickly as possible to get back to a matter-of-fact stance. Yes, of course your visitor may voice his or her views. It is important that you hear them. You would *like* to hear them.

Keep it informal. Even though the initiative for this meeting is with the visitor, it is within your power to set the tone. And in almost every case, a friendly, informal manner will be most conducive to a helpful exchange.

Of course, to some extent your role is a reactive one. If the protest is made under the pressure of considerable emotional steam, you may have to make a large effort to minimize the visitor's anger before you can begin the optimal calm exchange. Perhaps the best thing you can do is ask for time before responding. After all, the very nature of the situation makes it possible for you to put off immediate reactions or judgments; the dissenter has presumably approached you after giving some thought to the matter involved, whereas as far as you're concerned the whole business comes as a surprise. Arriving at a reasoned judgment clearly might *require* considerable thought and some investigation.

The Listener's Double Role

The position of the organization's representative may be as demanding and complex as that of the dissenter. Despite the appearance of solidity, of a person holding all the cards, the individual who hears a protest runs up against problems both psychological and organizational that can be difficult. It is generally accepted that the chair of judgment is a rickety piece of furniture. This case is no exception.

One might think that there is a lopsided power relationship between the dissenting executive and the one who listens to the complaint. The dissenter seems at a disadvantage, a supplicant before a judge, while the executive conducting the hearing seems backed by the authority and might of the organization. To use a poker analogy, the listener seems to be sitting with a pat hand, while the protester must draw cards to get something going.

The fact is, both protester and listener are likely to register some degree of mental stress. The situation of the dissenter has been described in some detail; let's look now at the equally complicated position of the organization's representative.

To put the matter simply, there is a duality to the listener's role, since he or she is on the one hand a representative of the organization, and on the other, a human being with personal values that may not coincide with those of the organization on the points in question. Thus, the protester is facing an individual who may be of divided mind, and accordingly will be listening with mixed feelings. To illustrate the pressures that may be at work on the listening executive, note the situation of a division manager whom we shall call Helen Patrick.

Helen gets a call from a subordinate manager, Grace Phelan. "May I see you for a moment?" "Yes, right now is okay."

A few minutes later, the two women face each other across the desk. Grace says, "Helen, I understand you're planning to give Wanda that job of research assistant. I told you a couple of weeks ago that I'd very much appreciate it if you'd give my sister-in-law that spot. She's had a lot of relevant experience and I'm sure she can do the work. And, frankly, for family reasons it's very important to me that she be hired."

Helen regards the manager for a moment and then says, "I've looked over the resume you gave me very carefully, and I don't think your sister-in-law's experience is suitable. If I thought there were a chance I would have asked her to come for an interview. But I think it would be a mistake for both her and the company to put her in a job she'd have trouble with."

Grace shakes her head. "All right, Helen, I'll admit that there might be some problems at first, but she'll catch on soon enough. The point is, as I've said, this is extremely important to me for family reasons. You've just got to give her a chance."

Helen folds her hands. "I'm sorry, Grace, the decision is already made."

Grace stands up. "I can't accept that, Helen. There are some things more important than just strict efficiency."

Pressure on the Company Representative

Keeping in mind the meeting between Helen Patrick and Grace Phelan, consider some of the pressures that an organization's representative may encounter in a confrontation with a dissenter:

Organizational interests. Basically, the listener, as a representative of the organization, must heavily weight his or her thinking on the basis of "what's best for the organization." While in the course of discussing a protest, the question of just exactly where the organizational good lies may evolve from the argument. At the outset, at any rate, the view of the organization in terms of a particular policy or decision presumably has been established, and it is this that the listener is supposed to defend and justify.

In a typical case an emotional involvement exists because of the listener's identification with the organization and acceptance of its ways and values. The executive should be aware of this, if for no other reason than to try to temper partisanship with some degree of objectivity.

Personal values. The listener may completely accept the prevailing organizational view. But it is also likely that, having personal principles and values, he may be somewhat at variance with the official dogma, in which case he is being called on to act against his own feelings. In the situation above, Helen Patrick could very well have been moved by Grace Phelan's appeal, and reconsidered the decision to hire on the outside. She might have agreed that "There are some things more important. . . ."

Clearly, how objectively the listener carries out his or her role is a major key to the constructive handling of dissent. But it is helpful to note that regardless of the mental outlook of the listener, whether calm or turmoil reigns, whether the general opinion is that the organization's view is correct or incorrect, there are still only a limited number of ways for a judgment to go. These are taken up in Part II, "The Five Ways Organizations Handle Dissent."

CHAPTER 4

The Dissenter—Traitor or Patriot?

One executive tells another, "I understand Burke is in the Old Man's office this minute protesting his dropping Paul Gallard and Henry Stitch. Isn't that great?"

SUCH reactions illustrate the polarization that may accompany protest. Those who agree with a protester may consider him a hero, those who disagree see the dissenter as a devil's agent who is about to threaten their views, their jobs, or do damage to the organization they hold dear.

Just what, then, does being "a dissenter" mean?

Why—and at what cost—does an executive break away from accepted views and values and, in effect, challenge the entire organization?

- Why does an executive start a course that may be rewarding or painful, and yet, perforce he or she "can do no other"?
- What about company loyalty?
- And having acted, where does the individual stand in the management's list of bad guys and good guys?

The answer to what the dissenting executive represents—from the viewpoint of his or her organization, colleagues, and own personal values—lies in the motives, risks, rewards, and personal costs of assuming the dissident role. We can learn a good deal about dissent by examining the ways in which the dissenter is regarded in the organization.

A Question of Perception

There are all kinds of dissenters. They may be good people or bad, selfish, self-sacrificing, unreasonable, heroic—any kind at all. But dissenters are rated not by their character but on the nature and outcome of the protest. And these evaluations tend to be highly subjective, reflecting the personal interests of the spectator.

The protester who risks his future in taking on the company may be acting on the highest principles. In protesting a decision that is seen as unethical, the dissident may be risking personal well-being for the greater good. But what if instead of furthering organizational good the protest threatens, or seems to threaten, the stability of the organization? In these days of environmental awareness, this is a very common dilemma.

For example, an executive takes issue with a company practice of flushing chemical waste into a nearby stream.

"We've been operating this way for 50 years," responds a management representative.

"But the amount of waste has increased drastically in recent years," counters the dissenter. "Now we are doing severe and irreparable damage to the wildlife that lives in and around that stream. I say we should stop at once."

"If we do as you suggest," the listening executive says, "we'd have to shut down that entire process. A thousand people would lose their jobs."

The ecologists might aver that the dissenter should push the protest, and so become a hero. But to the employees who would lose their jobs, and to the others in the organization who might suffer, the dissenter would seem a traitor.

It is sometimes argued that the better employee is the individual who seeks the good of the organization regardless of—one might even say in spite of—ethical considerations. Thus, an individual might disagree with a purportedly ethical decision that he or she thinks will threaten the organization's well-being. For example, Jack Brand protests to his boss, "We just can't dump that lot of cooking oil. It's not up to standard, but we can't take the loss."

The fact is that no black-and-white basis for judging the treason or patriotism of a protester is possible. However, this doesn't mean that there are no clear-cut cases where the morality or villainy of the protester can't be readily established. In one instance, an executive named Dave Noyes insisted that the company end its policy of selling prestige items that are losing money, and instead push a new line just developed in R&D. After a big hassle, Noyes carries the day. The organization zooms out of a slump, and suddenly everything from cash flow to the company's stock looks beautiful. Noyes is a hero.

Next, take the case of a "do-gooder." Dick Garvey pounds on the president's desk and says, "J.D., you've got to shut down that Riverside plant. The high incidence of chemical poisoning. . ."

"But Dick, the tests don't show any cause-and-effect relationship. We've had the government chemists in . . ."

"I don't give a damn. I don't need elaborate studies to tell me that we're risking the health of our employees."

Garvey gets his way. The plant is shut down. Next day, a group of bitter unemployed workers picket in front of his house. At work, no one talks to him. In his own mind, Garvey may be a hero. To fellow employees, he's a. . . .

The Pain of Dissent

For most individuals, taking up a combative stance against the organization is an ordeal undertaken only after considerable soul-searching. The reasons for the difficulty lie in the relationship between an individual and the organization with which he or she is affiliated. The very concept of membership—whether in a church, social club, or family—suggests involvement and identification. This sense of belonging brings with it a pattern of related feelings: you are instinctively loyal to an organization which you have become a part of; you defend it, right or wrong.

One of the most important alliances, of course, is with one's country. People give their lives to defend or otherwise help their native or adopted land. The most courageous and idealistic feats have been performed out of a sense of patriotism. In a similar way individuals identify with the organization in which they work. As materialistic and generally uncaring as we are said to have become, it is seldom that one encounters an employee without some identification with the organization that has taken him or her in, particularly at the executive level.

This is not to say that one does not hear criticism—and sometimes of an extremely bitter nature—against the establishment. But even when the bitterness and criticism are at their height, there is often a sense of regret. Most individuals would rather be in tune with the organization than see it as "the enemy."

Ties to the Organization

An employee in conflict with the organization on which he depends for his livelihood is in a difficult emotional situation. The stresses arise from the basic nature of the employee-employer relationship. When a person is hired there is an immediate interdependence set up between him and the organization. Of course the nature of this relationship is subject to change. In the early years of the Industrial Revolution, for example, the relationship of employee and employer was not unlike that of a slave and master. With time came a more enlightened and equitable relationship. Somewhere along the way there developed a paternalistic relationship. There was a quid pro quo: In return for obedience and loyalty the organization would "take care of" the employee—pay some attention to his well-being, in addition to handing over a check.

In recent years the relationship has continued to develop, reflecting present-day realities. Company loyalty as such has generally disappeared from the business scene. In its place there is a more realistic bond. The worker is convinced that he is worthy of his hire. He is there because the organization needs his services. And the organization, realizing it has a responsibility for the individual's well-being, offers fringe benefits of various kinds and in most cases takes a real interest in the individual's welfare. The fact that a satisfied worker is likely to make a greater contribution to the organization than a dissatisfied person may or may not be incidental.

Whatever the particular circumstances may be, as an employee's tenure increases, so does the emotional bond. The bond is further strengthened as the individual gets closer to the higher management levels, and as his view of company goals becomes a matter of greater personal concern.

The true nature of the employee–organization tie becomes clearer when it is broken or threatened. According to one authority, Dr. Lloyd Hamilton, a New York psychologist, "Employees who suffer most when they lose their jobs undergo some kind of severance from a figure on whom they were emotionally dependent. It may have been an esteemed superior, a mentor within the company. In some cases the company itself plays the role of protector.

With this prop gone, a feeling of loss and helplessness results, and a host of fears are mobilized."

The dissenter, particularly when he initiates active protest, risks the disturbing feelings that come from injuring the organizational bond. In addition to the loss of belonging, as suggested by Dr. Hamilton, there is a threat of repercussions ranging from the ill will of one's boss to being fired or having to quit. And in between are such penalties as a decline in one's standing and a loss of rapport with other employees.

Some authorities see the emotional difficulties of the executive dissenter as resulting from role conflict, that is, the dilemma of having to play two roles at once: a loyal member of the organization—indeed, part of its management—and an individual with distinctly personal views and values. The process of protest brings those two roles into conflict, frequently resulting in emotional upset.

Sources of Reluctance

A number of undesirable, potential consequences give the would-be protester cause to hesitate. They are considerations like the following:

Fear of failure. Taking on the establishment usually means standing up against the odds. The dissenter is always confronted by the traditional warning, "You can't fight City Hall." Obviously you *can* fight City Hall; the point is that the odds of actually forcing constructive change are painfully low.

Damage to one's "membership." For the most part, being a dissenter makes one a loner, a standout—a fly on a white wall. One becomes the center of an uncomfortable spotlight. Unlike the natural rebel, for whom this feeling is part of the gratification, many individuals find that being seen by the public as a dissenter means an unwelcome loss of acceptance in the group and the social standing that goes with it. In some cases protest leads to:

Ostracism. Society has always had ways of handling individuals who are in disfavor. They are committed to an emotional Siberia, kept there by a ring of disapproval or silence. The executive boat rocker, then, may experience not only defensive behavior on the part of his fellow employees, but ostracism as retaliation for the threat they feel.

This rejecting behavior may be harsh and obvious, or mild and subtle. In the former case, the dissenter may be made uncomfortable to the point where quitting becomes imperative. Should this be the dissenter's move, it will cast him in the role of traitor in some people's minds, and as a hero to the others.

But even though extreme reactions are unlikely, the consequences tend to be negative, and add to the personal ordeal of the dissenter. You are not apt to find your office door painted with tar, nor is there likely to be a conspiracy to avoid you. What is likely is that amenities previously taken for granted are either watered down or disappear. Friendly relations with peers somehow cool off. Invitations for lunch with colleagues peter out, and when the dissenter takes the initiative everybody seems to have a full calendar.

It is as though you become a half-person. You're still there and some of the relationships and group activities continue, but even in work-related matters you find that your anti-establishment reputation has lessened the helpful responses and cooperation you used to count on.

But let's not overdo it. It's important to remember that in many cases the dissenter finds allies and adherents—among colleagues at various levels—boss, subordinate, and so on. The backing may range from a quiet affirmation to a raucous backslapping. It happens often that the dissenter who strikes a popular note, who takes a stance that has the approval of others, winds up at the forefront of a crusade. He or she becomes the hero rather than the bum.

Alienation. Almost all of us have a great need for belonging. This emotional craving, ranked prominently in Maslow's hierarchy of needs, is a precondition for peace of mind in all but a few of us. To some people the need to identify with the organization, to stay within its warm and protective embrace, is a powerful consideration. To be unaffiliated may create a sense of aloneness that is frightening.

Material losses. A particularly strong restraining force is the possibility that one's value to, and future in, the organization will be irrevocably diminished. In many cases this is the single most powerful deterrent to dissent. People who feel that opposition to the establishment is likely to damage their reputation or impair them professionally are going to think twice before taking action. And of course, if there is a possibility of getting fired, dissent is reduced to a truly desperate act. The issue, in that case, would have to be highly important to the protester.

The Two Positive Motivators

Winston Churchill said, "Whenever someone comes to me who is in a controversy and says, 'It's not the money, it's the principle of the of the thing,' believe me, it's the money." You may or may not buy Churchill's cynicism. But his statement does embody the two general issues that impel an individual to assume the protester's stance.

Principle

We all have ideas and assumptions by which we live. Many or even most of them are buried in our subconscious. And we may be as surprised as anyone to discover what they are.

A social commentator once said, "A man might live out his whole life in the twentieth century without discovering whether or not he were a coward." It's also true that an attitude can be firmly locked in our minds, but remain hidden as long as it is not hard pressed. You become a protester when a situation develops that causes you to become aware of that attitude or principle. It may simply be the love of justice, or a strong feeling that your idea is better than the establishment's. In some cases it may not stem from a principle, but a champing at the bit over inaction.

The person who has an impulse to make an assertion, to push for a particular point of view, pays a penalty for *not* acting on his feeling. The penalties are frustration, a sense of impotence, and a feeling of being exploited. It is these kinds of feeling that can precipitate action and engender a healthy tendency to put one's mouth where one's principles are.

Personal Gain

Let us not forget the advantages that may accrue to good old number one in taking up the cudgels. There are all sorts of ways you can benefit from dissent. On the one hand, there is the satisfaction of being right—in some ways the sweetest reward of all. Another gain may be greater respect and admiration from one's colleagues and even from higher management. For although management may not always take kindly to protest, it does tend to view favorably the person who shows initiative and assertiveness—two qualities that the protester can't help but show.

When the protest is over a particularly moral issue, success brings special status to the dissenter. He may become a hero to others, a white knight in his own eyes. This ego-boosting for some individuals may be a major incentive, and if this is the case, the ego-involvement may take the protest out of the matter-of-fact category and may make it a crucial concern for the protester. In this case, the protester is playing for high emotional stakes that may distort the practical aspects of what is involved and the rationality of protest. At the same time, the desire to win—whatever the stakes—can neutralize all other considerations.

Judging the Dissenter

There are probably as many ways of viewing a protester as there are people. Still, it is possible to sift out three key criteria:

The justice of his or her position. Perhaps wisdom, reasonableness, or humanity are more relevant here than justice, but what they all add up to is whether the stand the dissenter takes is morally, economically, or technically superior to that of the establishment. Is it more fair? Is it more reasonable? Does it include more consideration for the human elements of the situation? What are the social aspects of the matter? The ethics?

Motivation. The driving force of the dissenter may be critical in his gaining support. If you like your heroes pure and high-minded, then a dissenter who has no thought of personal gain, but is arguing from principle, will draw at least your implicit backing. A protester who is pushing for personal benefits, seeking self-aggrandizement of a political nature, is apt to be seen as having his toe in the door of the traitor's club.

Consequences. The results of a protest may vary from constructive to destructive, with all manner of intermediates. If the protest helps people, benefits the organization itself in some observable way—for example, a protest about inadequate air conditioning that results in a new system, making a whole group more comfortable—the protester is viewed positively. However, if the same protest comes to nothing, and only serves to cause a furor, the dissenter may well be viewed as a troublemaker.

A Delicate Balance

The individual who contemplates active disagreement with the organization is usually engaged in an internal war over contradictory feelings and values. The term "soul-searching" is an appropriate one for the kind of inner conflict that takes place. A long-standing acceptance and identification with the organization will have to bear examination and possibly be abandoned. Personal and professional status may have to be risked. Whatever the considerations, whatever the weight of the pro and con factors, the potential dissenter must eventually select a course of action from among three possibilities:

1. *Abandonment.* The individual decides that he or she is in the wrong and accepts the organization's view.
2. *Submission.* The individual continues to believe that his or her position is justified, but is reluctant to protest for fear of the consequences.
3. *Engagement.* The individual decides to assert his or her point of view, and register the dissent.

Each of these three courses has consequences, even though in the first two no action is taken. The reason is that in deciding you are wrong, or that you are right but can't act, you bottle up all sorts of tensions and injure your self-esteem. But engaging the organization in a protest involves a risk—a promise of gain with success, the possibility of loss in failure. The next chapter explores further the choices you face once the notion of dissent enters your mind.

CHAPTER 5

The Obstacles You Face—Best Friends Can Become Worst Enemies

Pauline Brand listens sympathetically
to her husband's description of shabby treatment
by his boss. "Why don't you tell him
where to get off?" she says.
"Remind him that the slaves were freed long ago."
Greg Brand shakes his head.
"I can't afford to lay my job on the line.
Because that's what'll happen."

THERE are countless ways of stopping or intimidating the would-be dissenter. If and when you are cast in that role, it helps to know what you may be up against, especially if you work for an unenlightened organization. Factors that weaken the impulse to protest derive from three sources: negative consequences, intimidation by others, and the organizational climate.

Negative Consequences

Many a dissident, after due thought, finds that the impulse to lodge an actual protest has dissipated. Here are some of the things that can throw a wet blanket on the fire of dissent:

Clear risks, questionable gains. Dissent is almost always a chancy matter. Though the protest is made to right a wrong, or to assert one's personal values in opposition to those of the organization, there may be ramifications that hurt the individual's position in the firm. Often these losses must be risked in the face of doubtful benefits. Even if management is swayed by the protest, you may end up with little in the way of victory, and yet the suspicion and ill will of your peers and superiors may linger.

Visibility. The act of making a contrary view known confers immediate distinction, though of questionable benefit: the dissenter stands out from all the others in the organization who go about their day-to-day affairs in the prescribed and accepted manner. Even if there's backing from like-minded people, the individual registering the protest is likely to feel as though he's being observed under a magnifying glass. You must decide whether you can take this. While it is said to be "lonely at the top," it may be even more lonely out on a limb—which is where the dissenter figuratively clings.

Commitment to a point of view. No matter in what terms the protest is made, it generally involves an assertion of an attitude or a principle. And the dissent, once made, may have the effect of permanently saddling the executive with that view.

In the short run, you may have no doubt of the rightness of your stand, but you might hesitate if you know that you'd be linked irretrievably with a particular partisan view. For example, you may think that full-line selling is a bad sales policy given the present situation. But if in saying you're against full-line selling now, everyone infers that you'll always be against it, you might want to keep your feelings to yourself.

"Rebel." The individual who protests may win the field, only to find himself or herself wearing a crown of thorns rather than of olive branches. Organizations, like individuals, can be poor losers. And the executive who has precipitated a confrontation and come out on top may thereafter, regardless of other deeds and performances, acquire the reputation of "rebel." It would be inaccurate to suggest that this reputation necessarily represents a handicap. However, in the normal course of organizational life, it is not likely to be a benefit. Damage to your career is a definite possibility.

Last step—out? The executive trying to decide whether or not to protest may have to consider the possibility that management may feel as though an ultimatum of sorts has been tendered: either it gives in to you, or out you go—whether you want to go or not. Of course you need not put the protest on an either-you-agree-or-I-quit basis. However, if you genuinely don't want to leave the company, you must be careful how you choose the context of your dissent.

At any rate, the dissenter, in considering whether or not to act, must give some thought to the judgment that is rendered. Conceivably, if the substance of a protest is agreed to, then the executive's position may be strengthened in the organization. But the executive who has protested and been overruled may suffer permanent damage in terms of anything from a loss of voice and effectiveness in organizational politics to being told that a resignation is in order.

Intimidation by Others

As in all situations involving interpersonal relations, the feelings of your underlings, overlings, and peers can affect your own thinking. Below are some of the common encounters that can give you pause:

Face-off. Protest requires that you meet an organization's representative, perhaps your boss, or another upper-echelon individual. In some cases, you may be called on to confront two or more executives at once. Such a meeting is likely to be tense and emotion-laden, particularly when the issue is touchy, or the stakes high.

For many people, it is this phase of dissent that weighs most heavily. Confrontation requires self-confidence and courage, and the ability to cope with emotion, your own as well as others'. It may be at this point that the dissenter is tempted to desist: "I'll wait for a better opportunity to go to the mat on this issue" or "I guess there are other people who have at least as much at stake as I have. Why should I be the one to beard the lion?" In moments of doubt, a tough boss may assume ogre-like proportions.

"Stendorf, are you loyal?" Tugs of conscience may stem from personal relationships. . . . In the golden age of silent movies, the mythical kingdom romance was a sure hit. In one such film, set in an imaginary kingdom of gallant men, beautiful women, and the usual scheming bad guys, the hero has a retainer named Stendorf, who sticks with his dashing master no matter what. And as a running gag, just before a risky bit of derring-do, the hero says to his follower, "Stendorf, are you loyal?" And Stendorf, by answering in the affirmative, would let himself in for considerable, punishing misadventure.

Similar tests—loyalty exams, as it were—are sometimes given in connection with dissent. For example, Cindy Geller feels she has a good relationship with her boss. In the three years of their association, they seem to have worked out a modus operandi which has resulted in mutual liking and respect. Hence, after some thought, Cindy has decided that there's no reason not to tell Guy Wilson exactly how she feels about a decision made in a meeting earlier in the day. "Guy," she says, "I think we'd be making a big mistake to increase the commission on the new line of electric brooms. It's bound to affect the sale of our other lines, and I intend to tell J.P. just what I think."

To Geller's surprise her boss jumps up angrily. "Cindy, I don't appreciate your coming in here with that kind of talk. I made it clear in the meeting that boosting the sales of the new line was not only important for the division, but would mean a great deal to me personally. After all I've done for you, the least I expect is loyalty."

In any situation where plans are judged not simply on their potential for profit or loss but also on the basis of whether they will further or hamper the fortunes of individuals or cliques, the element of loyalty is apt to be used to keep people in line. In the case just described, Geller would have to rethink her whole position in the face of Wilson's reaction of personal outrage. "After all I've done for you. . ." may be a difficult argument to set aside.

When a colleague gets personal. In some situations a reaction from a peer can prove as much of a deterrent as that of a boss. For example, an executive named Ed is having lunch with Henry, a fellow manager with whom he has a deep and friendly relationship. In the course of their conversation Ed reveals a disagreement with a view of Henry's and makes it clear that in a forthcoming meeting he intends to argue in opposition.

"But I thought you were on my side," says Henry. "You're the best friend I have in this whole outfit, the last person in the world I would expect to bring up objections."

Now Ed faces the dilemma of having to choose between friendship with a colleague and the need to satisfy his own integrity.

Sparks on the home front. Erica Brewster says to her husband, "Bob, I understand your feelings about your job. But I certainly hope you're not going to go complaining to Mr. Gill."

Brewster looks at his wife in disbelief. "But I just told you, I can't stand the gaff any more. The whole situation has become an intolerable mess of pettiness and backbiting."

"Too bad. But Jane Clark went through hell while her husband was out of work, and I won't have you subjecting our family to that."

It is clear—however you feel about the Brewsters—that a spouse or other family member may speak out against a protest. And when the family's opinion is relevant—after all, Mrs. Brewster does have a stake in her husband's job situation—the would-be protester must take that view into account.

Organizational Climate

The organization itself may engender passive but intimidating action stoppers. In the short list that follows, notice that the stifling influences tend to be structural rather than personal. This can make dissent all the more frustrating, but also more worthwhile in the long run.

Tradition. Some organizations have created a climate in which dissent and protest seem jarring, out of place. As in the Crystal Palace situation (see Chapter 8), organizations can create a climate of work in which harmony prevails and where rocking the boat seems as misplaced as cursing in church. The would-be protester in a company of this sort might find it particularly difficult making contrary views known.

The "City Hall" syndrome. One of America's more unfortunate political cliches—unfortunate in the sense that it is true—is that you "can't fight City Hall." The fact is it's difficult for an individual to take on the entrenched force of any bureaucracy. And once the upper echelon of management is viewed as a self-protecting and self-righteous entity, it becomes unlikely that you will undertake anything even vaguely resembling an attack. In short, as long as you view the higher management as "the enemy," you may well hesitate to do battle, regardless of the worthiness of your cause.

Harmony, every working day. It is assumed that organizations work best in a spirit of harmony. When Production and Sales pull in the same direction, customer satisfaction and profits tend to peak. When a boss and a subordinate see eye to eye, the work advances smoothly. Where the idea "harmony is beautiful" prevails, dissent almost always gets a bad name—and an unsympathetic reception.

But let's hold on that thought for a moment. Is harmony really so crucial an element of the work scene? Two observations raise questions about tranquillity as a business asset: first, successful organizations often show a briskness, and an almost snappish competitiveness between individuals, departments, and divisions that seems to sharpen the edge of endeavor and achievement; and second, if you analyze situations in which friendly, cooperative relations exist, it turns out that the benefits are often confined to *ongoing operations,* and do not apply to the long-range health of the firm. That is, cooperation seems to help get the work out. In another aspect of organizational life, that of *growth and change,* the factor of disagreement, dissent, and protest can act as a stimulant.

Styles of Harmony

A good deal of clarification emerges from the understanding that harmony is not a single state but may exist in several variations. For example:

There can be a pseudo-harmony, an enforced state with a smooth surface and a bubbling mess of dissatisfaction and repressed feelings underneath. Dissent is viewed as a hostile act. But there is another type of harmony which seems at first glance to be anything but peaceful. Argument and disagreement appear to dominate communication. But below the surface there is an accord among the employees based on strong involvement and acceptance of organization objectives, and on the understanding that people may say and do almost anything they like as long as the organization's welfare is the primary goal. This kind of harmony is not disrupted by dissent. Dissenters as a group are viewed as "the loyal opposition." Dissent is made—and accepted—as an attempt to expedite the achievement of company objectives.

Moments of Truth

Considering whether or not to rock the boat is likely to be a balancing act, as you weigh the reasons for and against making a protest. Certain aspects of this thought process may be completely rational and easily resolved. For example, you may be able to say, "I feel strongly about this matter. I know exactly how much it means to me, and how much of a risk I'm willing to take to have my say." But a considerable amount of the cogitation may deal in ambiguous issues and ambivalent feelings. In the case of Cindy Geller, for example, if she were to give in to her boss's demand for loyalty, how much would that frustrate her other feelings?

Sometimes the issue involves feelings that are not easily identifiable. For example, an individual may be shy or find it difficult to be assertive. And just when he gets an impulse to take issue with some company policy, he grows fearful of the confrontation and concludes "Oh, well, I guess it's not worth making a fuss." But his feelings linger, camouflaged by his timidity.

But behind that conclusion may be an array of pros and cons, both numerous and weighty, and even the individual himself or herself would find it difficult to view the conclusion and say, "I guess I'm giving up on this because I'm afraid to face my boss's anger—or his disappointment because I would not go along with him—or that I'd be afraid to lose my job, or the opportunity for promotion."

Not all decision making can be examined as a rational act. But the matters discussed in this chapter may assist the dissenter in those moments when the decision to protest or not hangs in the balance. But there is yet another factor to be considered, which is often the key to whether or not one becomes a protester: the mounting cost of silence.

CHAPTER 6

The Perils of Silence

THERE will always be more dissenters than protesters. Many an executive feels the urge to protest, but does nothing. Somehow, the impulse is put down by countervailing forces. Can there be any notable results from an unvoiced protest? Or does the impulse simply vanish like yesterday's idea, a gleam in the eye?

The fact is, the consequences of inaction are sufficiently profound to represent a major consideration in any discussion of protest. And since the consequences are damaging, for the most part, a reasonable person may well find this alone to be a powerful argument in favor of accepting dissent as a normal part of organizational function.

A phony atmosphere where everyone is in a constant pose of agreement and harmony is virtually certain to lead, sooner or later, to apathy among employees. Executives deprived of feedback from peers and subordinates tend to develop feelings of isolation and unreality. And perhaps worst of all, the nonprotesting dissident will begin showing physical and mental symptoms ranging from the inconvenient to the deadly, from headaches to high blood pressure and ulcers.

The Crucial Times When Nothing Happens

Inaction is normally not very crucial. We all have half-baked ideas which don't deserve to be followed up, or whims quickly deemed unworthy and then abandoned. But when you find that events put you in a position to disagree with your boss or management in some meaningful way, and considerations dissuade you from doing so, what occurs is not in the same league with "changing your mind" as when you switch your order from steak to lobster. What has likely taken place is an inner conflict between the impulse to assert one's self and the bottling up of that impulse.

The Andy Duff Case

As has been described elsewhere, the dissenter may face an array of dire consequences if a protest is made. But the decision to swallow one's feelings may also victimize the executive just as much. In the following case history, strong dissent is aroused which the executive decides not to voice to a higher authority.

"And now, folks," Bill Morgan says, "it is my pleasure to announce that as of the first of September my position as head of Sales will be taken over by Len Shaw. Everyone who has worked with Len will agree that he is the logical person to take on this job. As he will still report to me in my new position as vice president of Marketing, I will continue to have the privilege of working with one of the most capable sales executives I've ever known."

At the conclusion of the ceremony, the sales reps and home office sales staff—everyone from secretaries to division managers—crowd around to congratulate Shaw. That is, *almost* everyone. Andy Duff, an assistant sales manager, quietly ducks out the rear of the conference room and goes into his office, his face flushed. He closes the door.

Shortly, someone knocks and enters. It is Gwen Greely, Duff's secretary. For a moment the two regard each other, then Duff looks away. Exercising the prerogative of secretary and good friend, Greely says, "You should have been the first one up there to shake Shaw's hand."

"I hate that man's guts. They gave him *my* promotion!"

Greely nods. "I agree. It should have been yours."

"Well, then?"

"A shrug is sometimes the best move a person can make."

"Are you telling me I ought to simply accept this lousy deal?"

"Top management made the decision."

"Top management is wrong, dead wrong. We both know why Shaw got the job. He is Morgan's boy."

"If you feel that strongly about it, why not talk to Mr. Rawley? You're on good terms with him. Even if he won't reverse the decision, at least you'll put him on notice. And you'll get a load off your chest."

"I can't fight the bureaucracy."

"O.K., then. You still have all kinds of opportunities."

"I've just had my rump kicked. The best thing I can do is to start looking for another job."

"That's crazy, Andy. You have a good situation here. In the new setup you'll be second in command."

He shakes his head. "I'm going to start job hunting Monday."

Case Analysis

Let us roll back the camera to the point where Duff says, "Top management is wrong, dead wrong." Clearly, he is voicing dissent. But what happens next? Is he planning a protest with his boss? No. The disappointed assistant sales manager simply decides to quit, even though he has access to the company president, T. J. Rawley.

Why doesn't he protest? Certainly he's angry enough to want to register his feelings. The answer lies in the fact that Andy Duff is a dissenter but not a protester. He complains to a person with no authority, and so cannot exert influence. Top management will learn about his feelings after the fact, when he quits. Of course, there are those who'll argue that Duff was wise to quit, because he was unhappy and the situation could not be reversed. Seldom in business is an announced promotion revoked because of a rival's protest. And yet, though Andy may be correct in his assumption, he may be wrong in not following his secretary's suggestion to protest to the company president. As will be seen, in protest there is health, in silence the possibility of unpleasant consequences.

In Place of Protest

In many cases where there is dissent, but the executive feels there is no way to voice his feelings, protest may be made tacitly. Consider the following examples.

Departure. As in the Duff case, the executive decides to quit, but only after making his feelings known. In many such cases, the executive is really hoping to be asked to stay. He wants reassurance, not a new job. And sometimes he'll get the pat on the back. Other times, however, an executive will offer to resign to show the strength of his feelings about the issue. And to his surprise and disappointment, management doesn't try to prevent the separation but merely indicates that it will receive the resignation "with regret." So the executive has made a point—but at considerable career cost.

Vandalism. Dissatisfied employees sometimes make their protest by defacing or destroying organization property. Graffiti and theft are common. In the executive echelons, unhappy employees may abuse their expense accounts, or let some piece of company property go to waste by "accident" or "oversight."

Sabotage. The ultimate act of protest, intentional destruction of organization equipment, became practically *de rigueur* in the early years of the Industrial Revolution. In modern executive circles, self-throttled protest has been known to result in embezzlement, in setting fire to boxes of company records, and in erasing the firm's computer tapes.

Foot-dragging. In this type of tacit protest, the employee performs work in an inferior fashion. In some cases, the poor performance may actually be unintentional, the indirect result of a sag in morale. Another possibility is that the employee intends the below-par performance to be interpreted as a sign of his or her dissatisfaction. All of these tacit protests are destructive. And since they stem from a feeling that protest will be ineffective, it seems logical that a management hoping to avoid such consequences would, at a minimum, adopt a policy that ensures a fair and attentive hearing to the executive protester.

Choices Open to the Protest-Swallower

The consequences described all involve actions in place of protest. The dissent is not voiced and in its place comes behavior that is, to one degree or another, negative and destructive. It may be argued that a quit could mean a better job for the dissenter, eventually. Even where this is the case, the dissenter leaves behind some damage—withered hopes for a future with the organization, possible impairment to it.

But there are two other possible consequences which, neither satisfying nor outrightly injurious, happen very often in the real world.

Temporize. The individual may accept a policy or decision, but try to wheel and deal for some personal advantage. In Andy Duff's case, he might attempt to reinforce his situation, rebuild bridges, and reset his sights with the expectation that a new opportunity will arise for the position he is seeking. In At least it suggests constructive action. Or, a raise may be asked for, or a fancy-sounding title.

Submit. The executive may decide after a lapse of time to stifle his dissent and go along with the situation. This can happen wholeheartedly or grudgingly. In the latter event a wound remains which festers and acts as a drag on the individual.

The Price of Submission

The half-hearted submission is of special interest, since it is a major hazard both for the individual and the organization. Here is an example of what can happen.

Grace Birchwood was an assistant purchasing agent for a paint company. After two years in the purchasing department she got to be excellent at her job, an expert at digging up sources for hard-to-get supplies, resourceful in helping her company acquire materials at a good price.

Staying late to catch up on paperwork one evening, Birchwood came across a contract for a major purchase. She read the terms casually and then more closely. She saw that the contract tied the company to the supplier in such a way that it ruled out any chance of switching to another source. In effect, the supplier had an exclusive deal, and the prices seemed excessively high for what was being delivered.

The implication seemed clear: the contract was a rip-off on the company and in order for it to have gone through, someone had to have been bribed. She began to put other pieces of the puzzle together—snatches of conversation, unexplained meetings between her boss and others from the front office. She was sure they added up to flagrant dishonesty. She had to tell someone, to make the facts and her feelings known.

In the days that followed, Birchwood gave considerable thought to her discovery. In one way or another her boss had to be involved in the dishonesty she was sure was taking place. Even though little of this involved her directly—confined as she was to mostly routine work—she still felt extremely uncomfortable. In addition to a general revulsion against dishonesty, was her anxiety that the fraud would one day be discovered with disastrous consequences for her boss and others in the company whom she had, until this incident, held in high regard.

She worked with a sense of being surrounded by double-dealing. She tried to tell herself not to worry—after all, she wasn't personally involved. But this was not enough to lessen her feelings of guilt and fear. Much as she tried, she couldn't get up her courage to the point where she could confront either her boss or the other front-office executives she knew.

Birchwood thought it might be a good idea to start looking for another job, but nothing turned up that paid the salary she was earning. And so she decided to forget about that evening with the books which had made her privy to the off-color dealings.

But the body can be a relentless critic of the mind's activities. Birchwood shortly thereafter developed a sore back. Her internist recommended a specialist, but several visits to him proved useless. A highly respected neurosurgeon said that only an operation would help. Birchwood rejected this idea, although she was in constant pain and had to spend a good part of her weekends in bed.

By chance a friend told of an opening in his company's purchasing department and Birchwood applied. She got the job and one week after beginning her new position, the back ailment disappeared.

Reasons for Silence

From time to time executives find themselves in situations that resemble Grace Birchwood's. They are locked into an untenable position and, ruling out protest, they swallow their dissent. To explain their behavior to themselves, they try to convince themselves of rationales like the following.

- *Helplessness.* "There's really nothing I can do. I don't pack enough clout." Or, "Whatever I do it'll only make things worse." This was more or less what Birchwood felt.
- *Inferiority.* "The others must be right." It may be your boss or just your peers who represent the opposition, but somehow they are intimidating psychologically.

- *Adverse labeling.* "I don't want to be known as a troublemaker." People often shy from rocking the boat because they don't want to be considered as negative types. Protest is seen as antigroup, and the individual lacks the ego to oppose the establishment.
- *Unassertiveness.* "I just can't stand up to those V.P.s." People who feel they should protest and don't, may end up feeling like a failure. A feeling of impotence takes over. Damage is done to the ego, to one's sense of self. And such self-repression can be insidiously harmful, as Birchwood's case illustrates.

Silence as a Disease

Silence is supposedly golden. But it weighs like lead when it represents default of the right to protest. Not only is silence not golden, but, like a virus, it can lead to all kinds of unpleasant symptoms associated with psychosomatic ailments: upset stomach, headaches, ulcers, unremitting anxiety.

While medical authorities, even those who specialize in executive health, seldom explain stress as resulting from stifled protest, there seems little doubt as to the connection. One medical man observes, "The people subject to the most stress are those in the middle. They have no control over the changes they must put into effect." "No control" equals no action, which is the situation our nonprotesting dissenter finds himself in.

Dr. Harry Levinson, a management consultant on psychological problems, points out the results of holding back anger, which so often accompanies unvoiced protest.

> Some people are past masters at overcontrolling their angry feelings. The man who is always clapping a lid on his anger, pretending to himself and to others that he does not have any anger, constantly holding it within himself, is a good candidate for psychosomatic illnesses. He is like an automobile driver who is racing the motor with one foot and applying the brakes with the other—most of the time. A man who is constantly sitting on his own feelings loses some of the sparkle, spontaneity, and initiative he could have if he let himself be more free. To restrain or deny his feelings forces him to keep up his psychological guard continuously, an effort which requires much of his energy and literally wears some of his body organs, increasing the likelihood of such illnesses as hypertension, headache, coronary disease, and intestinal disorders. Repressed anger is an important factor in almost all emotional illness.*

The Load-off-the-Chest Value of Protest

Voicing dissent won't guarantee an emotionally healthy executive. But squelching dissent, ruling it out as a permissible form of expression is almost certain to keep medical people busy treating a parade of frustrated executives for everything from shingles to depression. Aside from all these horrors of silence, there is a yet unmentioned, powerful argument for creating an environment of vigorous dis-

* Harry Levinson, *Executive Stress,* New York, Harper & Row, 1970.

sent. Eugene E. Jennings states the case within the context of executive autonomy.

> The capacity for autonomy greatly facilitates corporate life. Because the individual feels able to exert some control over his destiny, he is capable of entering voluntarily into organized life and making responsible decisions for others. By his own freedoms and choices, the autonomous executive can apply the rules of authority and organization. He is capable of conforming to the requirements and rules of his superiors and remains free to choose whether to conform or not. In executive language, this eventually means that he is not entirely a creature of his corporate circumstances. More precisely, it means that he applies a personalized style to problems of authority and organization and, thus, creates the necessary conditions of self-realization and acceptance.*

As Jennings intimates, the executive who is free to agree or disagree with organizational fiat is likely to be not only a better person as concerns himself but better for the organization as well.

Does the Organization Ever Punish Silence?

In almost every instance, the penalties for not making a felt protest are self-inflicted. Whether it is a prickly conscience, a loss of self-esteem, or a move to quit, the executive who takes an exception to management policy or procedure and fails to speak up punishes himself or herself for inaction. And off-

* Eugene Emerson Jennings, *Executive Success*, New York, Appleton-Century-Crofts, 1969.

hand, you might think that is the way it would always be. But here is an instance where the organization disapproved of a manager's *failure* to dissent—and eventually showed its disapproval in unmistakable fashion.

The president of a well-known corporation describes the fate of a manager in his organization who failed to oppose a bad idea:

> We discussed the potential of a new product that had some flaws. The manager was in the best position to spot these drawbacks, and to disagree with those who were pushing for the product. He didn't fight very hard against the item, and eventually supported the idea of producing it. We went ahead and got the item to the market, where it failed dismally. By then we decided that the manager had been right in the first place, but that his failure to stand up for his convictions, to clearly disagree with his superiors who backed the idea, was a major fault in judgment.

The record shows the acquiescing manager was replaced shortly afterward.

One implication of this unusual case: In weighing the decision to register a protest, don't overlook the possibility that while dissent may leave the dissenter a dead hero—in the sense of being penalized for bucking the organization—*failure* to dissent may end up with the mute executive being a dead coward.

In Part II we shall deal with a crucial aspect of the protest process: How organizations can respond to the executives who take issue with them, and how this dissent can be used for the benefit of all.

PART II

The Five Ways Organizations Handle Dissent

An organization announces a new policy, or old policies founder. An executive sees a reason to protest. A meeting is set up with someone in authority. The next move is up to the organization.

There are always the extremes—"Forget it. You're wrong, We're right." Or "You're right. What should we do to get the situation in line?"

In reality, there are five basic ways of handling dissent. These include domination, containment, capitulation, compromise, and integration.

In the chapters that follow, it will be seen that the methods are not equally desirable. Some are designed to eliminate or water down protest. Others reflect more enlightened attitudes. Undoubtedly most executives can supply from their own experience examples of dissent that reflect each of the five modes of response. Of course, none are necessarily right or wrong. The question as to their appropriateness depends largely on what is involved in the dissent. Also, an individual case may not necessarily be judged on its merits, for the listening executive or arbitrating group, being human, are sensitive to other, secondary factors. Several of these factors are described here:

Who is making the dissent? In the real world the rank-and-file employee and the president don't pack equal clout. An upper-echelon executive is more likely to get a receptive hearing and exert more leverage for change than the lower-echelon individual.

Even within the same echelon, two individuals may exert different amounts of pressure. The individual who has a persuasive personality or is a comer is more likely to effect change than an individual who is weaker or who is considered deadwood.

Presentation. The way in which a dissent is made also influences its effect. In some cases a well-reasoned, well-documented basis for protest may win the day. In another instance it may be the emotionality of the protester that becomes persuasive—or intimidating—and affects management's decision.

And, of course, an overly emotional protest may be a negative factor in management's considerations: "Once he started ranting, I simply turned off," says a top executive confronted by an out-of-control department head.

As a result of these and numerous other secondary factors, involving everything from the moral fiber of the organization's representative to the flexibility of the organization itself, the final response is determined. In the chapters that follow, a number of case histories are presented to illustrate each of the five possible organizational responses.

CHAPTER 7

Domination—The Jane Killian Case

DOMINATION as a means of handling dissent proceeds on the assumption that management is right—period. This assumption may result from two different premises, that dissent is destructive and undesirable, and that protest is without merit. Management doesn't have to take criticism from its executives because it is always right; protest, when it arises, represents either stupidity or lack of group-mindedness. Nonconformity is seen as a mental aberration or a character flaw. If and when a contrary view *is* aired, management simply goes through the motion of explaining or justifying its stand. The executive is supposed to agree, or else. . . . But domination can also be used less arbitrarily. Management may listen to the protest, evaluate it, and *then* conclude that it is wholly without significance.

Domination, then, may simply be the approach used to discourage protest. And as executives have the same potential for being wrong about issues on which they dissent as they do in other areas of judgment, management can exploit the executives' insecurities through heavy use of the domination response.

Domination in the Hands of Hardheads

In the late 1800s, when management was notoriously inflexible, dissent was marked by its rarity. When it did occur, it usually got short shrift. In a biography of Andrew Carnegie, an incident is described in which a subordinate of the steel magnate attempted to disagree with a statement he had made. "None of that, Billy," Carnegie said. And that ended the matter.

While authoritarianism has faded as a management approach, it has not vanished altogether. The well-known head of a large conglomerate, a man whose enterprise and methods of operation brought his name into the headlines frequently, is an example of the way contemporary business executives sometimes handle nonconcurrence. Here's a description of the executive, as told by a colleague.

"Hal was quite accepting of views that differed from his," said a colleague. "Sometimes he even seemed to encourage them. The person who disagreed came out all right as long as, in the end, he turned out to be wrong. But if he was right and Hal was wrong, he usually disappeared from the organization chart."

Hal's method is one that *seems* to leave room for dissent, but really doesn't. Other modern ways of squelching dissent exhibit even less finesse. Newspapers recently carried an item explaining why a state commissioner of education had run into difficulties in his job. "He tended to throttle discussion," said an associate. "If you disagreed with him you became a nonperson. No more first names. He would simply address you by your surname."

The Jane Killian Case—Protest Against Unequal Pay

An incident reported by a well-known authority of the business scene further illustrates domination as a way of dealing with protest. At the heart of this issue was sex discrimination which, at that time, was not illegal. The episode reflects the atmosphere and manner that accompany domination when it is used to suffocate protest rather than to air it. At the time of this incident Jane Killian was a slim, attractive 28-year-old trying to make her way up the ladder. Her story follows.

> From the inception of my career (if you could call it that) with that insurance company in New York, I had received two promotions. I think I was finally making $130 at the end of two years. Then this man was hired into the department at the entry level position I had come in at and at that time he was making $2,000 more a year than I was at my present level of the measly $130 per week. So I went into my boss's office and I said I'd just discovered that "there seems to be a discrep-

ancy in salaries." It so happened that the man had the same background—two years of college, he was the same age, he had almost exactly the same liberal arts background, the same work background—an exact duplicate of mine.

I told my boss that I knew this man was making $2,000 more than I was and I was supposedly two levels above this man—Why? His answer was: "Well, you have to understand this man is married and has a child to support." I said: "But don't you realize that's discrimination?" He said: "Oh really, Jane, I mean—that's ridiculous. You just can't possibly think that, now really!"

Well, you have to understand this man. It wasn't only his blatant discrimination. I'm afraid this is still not uncommon, but, as I said, he was a politician. He was constantly down in the board room explaining this marvelous new budget he had and what fantastic improvements. . . . He knew nothing about what he was talking about. Every time they would ask him a direct question, he'd get on the phone and he'd go: "Jane, could you come down and explain this to me?" I thought: "A real asshole."*

Case Analysis

The Jane Killian case is particularly interesting because the protester is a woman who undertakes a direct confrontation with her boss. The dozens of books on assertiveness training, the countless seminars on the subject all emphasize the difficulties women have in speaking up for themselves. In a

* George DeMare and Joanne S. Ginsberg, *Corporate Lives: A Journey into the Corporate World,* New York, Van Nostrand–Reinhold, 1976.

course entitled Women in Management, given by the author at the New School in New York City, the students, all women, concurred in their difficulties in taking on the role of dissenter in a business situation. It is of special value, then, to note just how this young woman executive handled her protest.

Jane Killian's presentation. Notice that Killian's conversation with her boss seemed to take place almost impromptu. Furthermore, her revelation of the basis for the protest—"this man was making $2,000 more than I was and I was supposedly two levels above this man"—has a strong accusatory tone. Even if the boss were a fool, as suggested by Killian's final epithet, it would be difficult for him to have avoided a defensive authoritarian manner.

The boss's response. Notice that the first reaction is defensive and self-protective—"You have to understand this man is married and has a child to support." And then when Jane responds by accusing him of discrimination, his response is simply to put her down. Absolutely no consideration is given to the merits of the case. This attempt to simply cover up the situation, to deny the problem exists, is often typical of the domination response to criticism.

The outcome. Given the characters of the two people involved, Killian's forthright approach and the boss's disinclination to even consider what was being said, the eventual outcome was predictable. Killian left the organization and went on to become assistant vice president of a bank.

As is usually the case, the use of the domination approach by management yielded little in the way of benefits. The organization lost a capable employee, and apparently learned nothing about how to improve its adaptability.

Domination tends to reduce the frequency of dissent. And when dissent does occur, it tends to be muted and tentative. An employee whose protest is pretty sure to be put down usually will swallow his complaints, even when this is relatively painful. This is not to say that the spirit of dissent is destroyed. On the contrary, the method of handling dissent may itself inspire more protest, for repression fuels resentment, which leads to dissension and as a last resort explosive protest—the stronger for being repressed.

Left Out—and Angry

Few changes in our time have been as revolutionary as the freeing of women from many of their traditional bonds. The social, economic, and psychological consequences of women's liberation will definitely influence the pattern of our future lives.

On the work scene, some of the results of recent anti-discrimination measures are already becoming clear. Federal legislation, represented by Title VII of the Civil Rights Act of 1964, prohibits job discrimination based on sex. And the nation's response has been to comply with the law—by and large. In case after case where women have claimed to be discriminated against, the findings have been in their favor. But even where women have seen the barriers removed, and have begun to rise into job levels where previously they had been barred, old habits and traditions linger and prevent true equality. What this means in practical, on-the-job terms is that women must continue to fight individually for personal job objectives.

Some women see the struggle to gain full acceptance in their organizations as more than a personal matter. Out of a social consciousness, or a more limited concern for fairness to their sex, countless women have reacted strongly to instances of unequal treatment. Dissenting from a decision or practice, they make their opposition clear.

In the Jane Killian case we saw how one traditional-minded organization dealt with a protest using domination in a purely authoritarian fashion. Following is another case, also involving a female executive, in which domination is used in an intelligent way.

The Case of Penny Lang

Penny Lang, in her early thirties, was department head of a company that sold American books abroad. She had started with the company as a secretary, and had inherited her managerial job on an emergency basis when her predecessor became seriously ill.

But Lang had already developed a good understanding of the business and its procedures. She handled the job with such obvious capability that the company president, after making a brief and unsuccessful attempt to find a replacement for his ailing manager, announced that Lang would become permanent head of the department.

Lang continued to grow in her job, augmenting her work with night courses in management. One day, intrigued by the popularity of assertiveness training, which had grown out of the women's liberation movement, she enrolled in a seminar given at a local university. She learned a lot—but perhaps not enough. As a result of attending the course, she became aware of a situation at the office that bothered her. She felt she was being left out of management meetings in which she had a right to participate. The more she thought about it the more upset she became. It seemed clear that management was discriminating against her because she was a woman. One morning there was a closed-door session attended by her boss, the treasurer, and the sales manager. Lang stewed. She suspected they were discussing business problems that were directly relevant to her job. The very sight of the closed door seemed like a personal affront.

She waited for her opportunity. As soon as the meeting was over and the other executives had left, Lang walked into the president's office and shut the door behind her.

"What's up, Penny?" he said.

"That's what I'd like to know. I've been meaning to talk to you about this for some time, Mr. Avery. It seems to me that although you've made me a manager, you're not treating me like one."

The boss leaned back. "What do you mean?"

"These meetings you've been having with Joel and Peter. . . . I'm trying to grow in my job. I think I'm performing extremely well but it seems to me you're treating me like a stepchild. And I hate to say this, but I think you see these meetings as a men's club."

Avery said, "Sit down, Penny. I'm glad you spoke up because I sure as hell don't want this to spoil our relationship or handicap you in your job.

"Yes, it's true that there have been meetings in

which you haven't been included. But I want you to understand that it has nothing to do with sex discrimination. You weren't invited because we weren't discussing anything directly related to your work. In a larger company I guess we'd dignify these meetings by saying they involved the making of top policy. And frankly, as important as you've become to this company, you're not presently at a level in which you need be concerned with these areas. Perhaps some day you will be, and I hope that will happen. But in this situation I think your feelings are based on misinformation. I hope you agree."

Case Analysis

The Lang example shows domination in its more productive aspect. Although Avery minces no words in putting down her protest, he has given her a good hearing as well as a reasonable explanation for the meetings.

Of the five basic types of response to protest, domination is probably most crushing, the most ego-damaging. However, as the last two cases show, it may be applied differently. In the Killian example, the protester's views aren't even considered. Management, the listening executive implies, is beyond reproach. And Killian is put off with, "Oh really, Jane, I mean—that's ridiculous. You just can't possibly think that. . . ." The fact that she *does* think it isn't even countenanced. On the other hand, Lang's reception is quite different. Though her protest does not get her exactly what she wanted, the domination technique is used in a fair and intelligent manner. The protester is told in reasonable, even sympathetic, terms why management's view of the matter is valid. Fortunately, more and more managements conduct themselves as did Lang's boss.

The second type of response available to management is described in the next chapter. The case in point is based on an autobiographical business novel that had considerable impact some years ago.

CHAPTER 8

Containment—The Crystal Palace Concept

SOME organizations don't want to be accused of using authority to squelch dissent, but still feel that dissent is undesirable. Rather than seek to eliminate it, they try to water it down into a form that can easily be dealt with.

As with domination, implicit in this approach is the notion that the organization is an irreproachable, faultless entity, never to be taken issue with because it can do no wrong. This concept of the icily correct organization above criticism was portrayed vividly in a biographical novel called *Life in the Crystal Palace,** which attracted considerable attention when first published.

* Alan Harrington, *Life in the Crystal Palace,* New York, Alfred A. Knopf, 1959.

The Crystal Palace Syndrome

In the novel, author Alan Harrington describes how he came into the employ of one of America's largest corporations despite his reputation as an anti-business rebel. Harrington didn't expect to last long in his job, but the anticipated firing didn't take place. On the contrary, and to his pleasant surprise, he was treated with courtesy and with great regard for his comfort and well-being.

His new boss has him in for a long talk: "We want you to be happy here. Is there anything we can do? Please let us know." Life in the organization is like an unpressured Lotus-land. A typical scene: an employee has done badly on an assignment; his boss tells him, "Next time, Walt, try it the other way." Walt subsequently tells Harrington, "Boy, I sure got a bawling out!" And Harrington never protests because there is literally nothing to protest about. The company seems surrounded by a protective gelatin that offers no issues with which to differ, no behavior about which to complain.

In organizations such as this, dissent is discouraged through its seeming so terribly *out of place.* In fact, Harrington himself winds up in a state of frustration as he realizes that individuality and self-assertiveness have themselves been undermined.

Case Analysis

Life in the Crystal Palace is so secure, so protective, and so bland that controversy and disagreement would be as out of place as scatalogical remarks in a funeral parlor. And protest, when made, is undercut by syrupy good will.

Organizations can be overly accepting, almost parental, so that the harder edges of reality—partisanship, competition, controversy—are lacking. And in this neutral, soporific climate, meaningful dissent is unlikely to appear.

The Crystal Palace atmosphere arises out of seemingly good intentions. But if attempts to oppose the organization are viewed merely as aberrations—the result of momentary grouchiness rather than serious disagreement—the organization will be denied the benefits of review and modification.

Total acceptance is undesirable because it reinforces the dissenter in a misleading, artificial way. Containment disregards the *content* of the dissent. In effect the protester is told, "Say anything you like, criticize, find fault, and we'll still love you—but don't expect us to take your protest seriously." The problem, of course, is that after a while you can't take the company seriously either.

The Crystal Palace approach seeks to minimize protest, sweep it under the rug. Organizational climate is such that dissent is made to seem an ungenteel act, a bad smell in the nostrils of management.

Other Methods of Containment

Protest can be contained many ways. While the Crystal Palace approach concerns a management-wide climate that is built up over time and across a broad front, containment can also stem from individual listening executives. Their approach may or may not reflect their personal views or management's thinking. In either case, one of the following tacks may be taken:

Pressure. "I ask you as a long-time friend. On the basis of our personal relationship, I ask you to forget about this issue." Whatever the wording, the organization's representative attempts to wall in the protester, to blunt his dissent by a personal appeal. Past friendship may be called on. Or the dissenter may be asked to accept the superior judgment of the other: "You know you can trust me. I wouldn't steer you wrong."

Fear of organizational damage. "Why, Gary, don't you see that if we tried to do what you advocate, we'd be out of business tomorrow?" Here, the listener argues that the dissenter must put aside his feelings because to push them would hurt the organization. This approach appeals to both company loyalty and the dissenter's own job security. If the listener can make a strong case to the effect that "If you succeed in having your view adopted, the damage will outweigh any possible benefits," there is no question that it would silence most protesters.

Fear of career damage. "Charlotte, I can tell you this. If I communicate your protest up the line, you'll surely ruin your career here." Dear to the heart of most executives is the shot at moving up in salary, status, authority. Any act that would tend to enjoin upward mobility would certainly be thought about twice. And on that second thought, a protest that would be resented by higher management is likely to be stifled.

Cost. Money, as they say in the world of business—and just about everywhere else—talks. And so, being told that an ethical consideration brought up by a dissenter would "cost more than the company could possibly afford" constitutes a strong argument for forgetting about it. Likewise, the suggestion, "We've got to stop using that cheap solvent because it seems to cause skin irritation" will clearly lead to increased costs. Now the question becomes, for both the dissenter and the listener, What constitutes a reasonable trade-off between worker safety and company dollars?

But containment doesn't make room for this rational and even necessary process. This is why containment can be most frustrating to serious-minded and involved executives. They are not given a response to the protest, but only emotion-laden reasons why the protest should not be made. It is fortunate, then, that it is probably the least used of the five ways of handling dissent.

CHAPTER 9

Capitulation—The Claire Elting Case

"YOU'RE making a good point," the organization representative says. "In view of your arguments it makes sense to stop what we're doing and try it your way."

This listening executive's statement exemplifies capitulation—when the dissenter's view is accepted. It represents the logical reaction when management has something to gain by giving in to the protester.

Usually, however, the dissenting view must be more than simply "as good as" the one that prevails. To be acceptable, it must be strong enough to overcome two obstacles:

Organizational inertia. It usually takes more effort to change direction than to keep things the same. Therefore a dissenting view must have sufficient appeal to overcome the deadweight of the status quo.

Managerial integrity. Management usually justifies capitulation only on the basis of possible benefits. In some cases these may be intangible—as when a dissenter's view is adopted because it seems more ethical or more just. Other times the benefits may be material, such as higher profits or greater productivity. Management is correct in thinking that the making and unmaking of decisions, adopting a policy and then abandoning it, brings management's will and wisdom into question. Nevertheless, as many a manager comes to realize, capitulation is a perfectly viable—even necessary—response to protest.

Hazards develop, however, when capitulation is seen as an expedient. Occasionally you will find an organization which seems to think that the best way to deal with dissent is to readily give in to it. In most cases this is unwise. An organization so lacking in self-confidence that it goes along with all criticism is seriously deficient in leadership. But, obviously, this does't happen very often. More common—though still somewhat of a rarity—are protesters with a unique relationship with the organization that makes capitulation the only logical response.

The Hard-to-Refuse Protester

Some dissenters, like the proverbial 800-pound gorilla, can get anything they want. These employees pack tremendous clout, and their views are accepted virtually automatically. And all of it may be justified. The engineering wizard, Charles Steinmetz, had a relationship of this kind with the

General Electric Company. Not only was he a highly valued individual whose genius helped G.E. make giant technological strides, but his suggestions concerning development were often right on track. Through sheer merit—not to take anything away from his personal charm—he could criticize virtually anything about the huge firm and usually get his way.

The status of the employee, then, is a key factor in capitulation. The protester needn't be a genius, or the president's relative; all he or she really needs is a level head, capable of coming up with a superior alternative. The following is a case at point:

"We changed our whole policy on supervisory training," a personnel administrator admits, "because of a manager's views. Ellen Ritchie came in and argued that we were wasting our effort on training sessions for our supervisors. She favored on-line training, with close liaison between the supervisors and the next higher level of management. After some consideration we decided that she was right. We tried it. Her approach turned out to be much more effective."

Capitulation need not be automatic or precipitous. When it is used effectively, it represents recognition of an employee's experience or wisdom, and a willingness on the part of management to be flexible and not overly enamored with its own way of doing things.

The Claire Elting Case

Claire Elting is a woman of 40, a college graduate who majored in economics and political science. Shortly after leaving college, she took a temporary job with a utility company. Ames Prater, president of the firm, needed help writing some speeches and putting together several articles for professional journals. He hired Elting on a friend's recommendation.

Her unusually high intelligence, along with her writing skill, soon became obvious. Prater couldn't have hoped for a better assistant. As a result, when the temporary job was over, he asked her to stay on and work in customer services and market assessment.

In a couple of years, Elting's abilities won her a management position as assistant to a division manager. When her boss was promoted to vice president, she was made acting head of the division. As she remembers it, "There was a brief pause while top management went into a huddle to decide what to do about this unprecedented situation. Should they—could they—really take the plunge, and make a woman division manager?

"I heard later that some of the arguments were pretty heated—'The staff won't accept a female boss. . . . There is a lot of pressure in that job, she'll cave in'—and so on, all the stereotyping you would expect.

"It was my ex-boss who had the last word. He said, 'She's the best person for the job.' He stuck to his guns, I got the promotion."

Elting's astuteness and her analytical abilities again reinforced her in her new job. Her department operated smoothly. From time to time she had difficulties with individual subordinates, but nothing out of the ordinary, nothing different from the problems of other managers. She seemed to have won complete acceptance from top management and from her peers. But she was aware of subtle barriers. Some of the signs stemmed from traditional male gallantry: in meetings, some of the men would stand when she came into the room. An occasional off-color joke would be preceded by "I hope Claire will forgive me if I tell the one about. . . ."

She used one such situation to make her feelings clear. When a male colleague apologized for using a common four-letter word, she said, "I really don't give a _____ what you say, as long as you express yourself clearly."

That incident made the rounds, and Elting got the impression thereafter that she was being treated with more real respect, and less male-chauvinistic pussyfooting. Years later, upon the blossoming of the women's liberation movement, Elting would jokingly say, "I guess I'm Prater's token woman executive."

The Queen Bee Syndrome

Elting could make light of the situation because she was now relatively secure in what would generally be regarded as a high-level, high-status job. Most people in her position would tend to soak up the benefits with as little rocking of the boat as possible.

Why play it safe? Because some women, once ensconced in positions of power, like the idea of being "the only woman around." Not only are they not eager to have other women follow in their footsteps, but they are opposed to it. Perhaps they fear that other women will give them undesirable competition, or that a poor performance on the part of another woman would reflect badly on her or on women managers in general. This attitude and the behavior that derives from it has been sufficiently prevalent for it to have drawn the label, the Queen Bee Syndrome.

Elting was not guilty of this. On the contrary, out of a sense of what was good for the organization and the justice of equal treatment, she steered clear of Queen Bee behavior, espousing women's equality whenever it seemed appropriate.

A Protest Against Bias in Business Clubs

One morning, an invitation crossed Elting's desk. It was on the occasion of the 25th anniversary of Ames Prater's association with the company. Prater, you may remember, was Elting's mentor. The affair was to take place off company premises, at one of the more prestigious clubs in town. This club was so tradition-bound that it still enforced a 19th-century practice of not allowing women to enter through the front door. And women were admitted to the club only under special circumstances, such as Prater's party—that is, when an organization rented the club's private dining rooms. Using the club's dining facilities, by the way, was a privilege only accorded club members, which included several of the top executives in the utility.

Elting understood the situation and decided to protest the site of the anniversary celebration. Accordingly, she sent a memo to Paul Warren, the personnel director who had issued the invitation.

TO: Paul Warren
FROM: Claire Elting
DATE: September 24, 1976

Dear Paul:

Thanks for your invitation to Mr. Prater's 25th anniversary celebration at the Turkey Club. Much as I would like to attend—you know the high esteem in which I hold him—I feel it is improper, as part of my job, to participate in activities at a club where I would not be welcome as a member.

I will not attend any company function that is held at a club which would not accept me or any other employee as a member because of my race, creed, or sex.

In addition, I would like to urge you to reconsider company policy in relation to these clubs. All of them can continue to operate only because they are supported by the dues and fees paid by businesses and businessmen who should be committed to ending discrimination.

In my opinion, a genuine commitment to affirmative action would require the company to withdraw support from any organization that discriminates. This would include both refusing to use the facilities and discontinuing the reimbursement of dues to employees who belong to such organizations.

As you may know, I am not alone in this position. The Treasury Department has recently questioned whether such reimbursements are a violation of the civil rights law. Whether or not it is a technical violation, it is certainly not in accord with the spirit and intent of the law. I hate to see our company in that position.

The protest was successful. Plans were changed and the affair was held at a hotel instead.

"It's not that I pack such terrific clout," Elting explained. "I believe that management simply was unaware that what was being done was wrong. Or if they did, they didn't feel anyone minded. Once I called attention to the facts, the justice of my view became clear."

It should also be said that Prater subsequently resigned from the club and suggested to other members of his staff that they follow suit.

Cleaning Up One's Own Back Yard

But woman's work is never done, particularly when she sets out to fight the good fight against discrimination. One morning a form arrived from Personnel headed, "Manpower Survey."

Elting reflected, "It's unbelievable how old habits and customs hang on. I know my company is sincerely dedicated to the principles of equality, but I'm not naive enough to believe that every male on the roster has expunged all discriminatory feelings from his mind. Something like a 'manpower survey' may not strike you as very serious, only to me it was the straw that broke the camel's back.

"I returned the form with a note to the personnel director, saying I would be happy to fill out a 'Personnel Survey' but the one devoted to 'manpower' would mean leaving out all the women in my department."

A Chink in Her Armor?

One day at lunch a colleague chided her for taking up a lot of token issues. "When it comes right down to it, Claire, you're not beyond taking advantage of members of your own sex."

"Why do you say that?" Elting couldn't comprehend the charge.

"Well, I know for a fact that you hired a writer for your promotion staff and although she had a lot of experience and was rather skilled, you started her at the lowest salary range."

Elting thought for a moment and then said, "What you're saying is partly true. I hired her at a lower salary, but only because that's what she asked for. After all, her starting salary to some extent reflected her previous earnings. But while we're at it, let me say this: I'd rather hire a woman at $15,000 than a man with equivalent skills at $20,000. That's just good business sense. But once she has proved herself I'll give her a raise as soon as possible that will put her on a par with the rest of the staff."

Case Analysis

Claire Elting provides some revealing insights into the role of the dissenter. In her case her protests reflect not only a personal and individual way of looking at things but also a vast social change. And within her corner of the world she was helping bring that change about. In her person, then, we see how dissent and protest can become a reflection of broader reforms in society.

Behind the Capitulation Response

At the beginning of this chapter it was pointed out that capitulation represents management's acknowledgment that the dissenter's way is the better way. When management has become sufficiently enlightened to recognize protest as a potential contribution to the organization's well-being, it follows that it will also come to see that the dissenter's view may actually replace that of the establishment.

Elting protested two different ways, and in both cases management capitulated. In each instance management agreed with the justice or propriety of the argument. But implicit in the capitulation is another fact about protest: it represents the means by which organizations change, adjust to new influences, achieve contemporaneity. Seen in this way, Elting's case serves well in demonstrating the dissenter's role as an agent for reform. Not only was she able to bring about changes in company practice but, because of the attitudes and values she stood up for, her organization became better equipped to deal with the future.

Capitulation as a Quantifier of Dissent

When management accedes to the protester, it may do so only to a limited extent—the degree to which the organization actually agrees with him or her.

Arthur Robbins protests to his boss that the decision to award a contract to a new supplier is all wrong. "Just because Consolidated performed poorly on our last order is no reason to drop them completely. The fact is, Consolidated has been a darned reliable source for us for a long time. And the outfit we're considering doesn't have that satisfactory as record. Those files I've shown you make the case better than anything else I can say."

Robbins's boss has several possible responses to give. But he chooses capitulation because he has been completely persuaded by the protester's arguments. This sort of reaction to protest is proper when management is entirely wrong or the dissenter is clearly right. If Robbins were only partially persuasive, and his boss was left with some doubts, a more likely response would be a compromise: "We'll switch for a few months and see what happens." But the boss agrees with Robbins that the decision to change suppliers is an over-reaction to a minor or temporary fault.

When the protester proves his or her contentions completely, a reasonable management may have no alternative but to go along. Capitulation represents unqualified agreement with the dissenter, management's considered judgment that the issue in contention is best settled by going along with the point of the protest.

Partial Capitulation

There is still another aspect of dealing with protest that arises from the capitulation response. An executive registers strong disagreement with some procedure or policy. Only it doesn't matter how well-founded the protest is, because for its own reasons management decides that it will give in—that is, it will *appear* to give in. The objective is to quiet the protester by, in effect, buying him off with a sham victory. "We're certainly not going to go along with what is being asked of us. But let's give just enough to keep him quiet."

Partial capitulation is not unlike compromise, the subject treated in the next chapter. It differs mainly in spirit. Partial capitulation is often merely a holding action. As such, it is insincere, an expedient rather than a true solution. Compromise, as you will see, is the more exemplary and acceptable result of a management acting in good faith.

CHAPTER 10

Compromise—Old-Timers vs. the Young Turks

COMPROMISE is attractive because it promises to yield the best of two possible worlds. Management seems to be behaving *fairly* to the dissenter and *responsibly* vis-à-vis itself. Presumably the worthy element in the dissenting executive's view is added to management's overall policy, with a resulting strengthened hybrid.

And this is indeed often the case. Compromise, when used wisely, can result in benefits to employee and management alike. But what frequently happens is that management adopts this approach as *the* way to handle dissent. Two problems may stem from this:

The process of dissent is weakened. If, no matter who says what, management is eager to be agreeable—"Yes, you are certainly right—not completely right, but you do have a point"—chances are management is not viewing dissent properly. And the dissenter, working in an atmosphere of this kind, is both put off because he doesn't really get a fair hearing, and is encouraged to look for other occasions to dissent, since there will almost always be acceptance of some kind.

Management develops a major ailment. The management of an organization is like an organism—the separate parts interact with one another, and an event in one area may affect the whole entity. For example, a wise policy decision in a matter as seemingly peripheral as the company parking lot can favorably affect the entire organization. A poor policy regarding a pension program creates uncomfortable stresses throughout. So when management adopts a method of handling dissent that is not really an effective approach, but merely an expedient, it spreads wholesale a feeling of make-do, of short-sighted pragmatism that ultimately harms the organization. Principle seems shaky, decision making even more so.

A Management Divided Against Itself

Dr. H. Jack Shapiro, Professor of Management at Baruch College, City University of New York, was called into consultation by a company in which dissent seemed to threaten the organization's survival. The dissent was being voiced not by one person but a group of mostly younger executives who were especially aggressive in terms of both promoting the company and advancing themselves professionally. That the case illustrates compromise as a way of handling protest was virtually predetermined by the inclusion of a third party go-between. The facts as reported in a well-known management newsletter* were as follows.

> The company, a manufacturer of sophisticated hydraulic components and systems for the military, started in business in 1951 as a five-person operation. For 18 years it had grown very slowly until its sales reached $2.5 million with profits of $175,000 before taxes. As a group, the president and "the old-timers" were strongly opposed to any risk ventures, and would have been happy to maintain the status quo. They said they favored growth, but in reality only at a snail's pace. Their outlook had been formed during the early years of the firm when it was struggling for survival. Their "safety needs" were clear and understandable.
>
> Primarily these people were in charge of the manufacturing, financial, and administrative functions. The personnel in marketing, sales, engineering, and contracting, however, were in constant conflict with the old-timers and pushed for accelerated expansion. They wanted more physical space, more sophisticated equipment, a research and development team, more aggressive sales and marketing. They realized that if they were to grow within the company, the company itself must grow. Their "personal needs," which sometimes led to aggressive behavior, were also understandable.
>
> By the late 1960's, this conflict approached the crisis stage, and the president feared that the

* *Interaction*, New York, February 16, 1977.

company's very existence might be threatened. With the assistance of the consultant, this program was devised:

1. *Open confrontation.* A long weekend was set aside for a "confrontation meeting" at which company goals, group goals, and individual aspirations were discussed without fear of reprisal or ridicule. Attitudes and feelings were listened to with respect and understanding. The problems were identified and analyzed. The president committed himself and the organization to working out a detailed plan to be presented at future meetings.

2. *Formulation of policy.* The premise of change was accepted by all. In subsequent meetings, the agenda was to spell out a policy and procedure that would *take into account the psychological needs of both sides.*

Diversification outside the company's present expertise was rejected since it was incompatible with the security needs of the veterans. A strategic plan of accelerated but controlled growth was held to be acceptable, satisfying the objectives of the younger people. To guarantee the safety needs of the more cautious older group, it was agreed to set up a financial reserve.

3. *Implementation—priorities and timetable.* The policy was then translated into specific targets, each of them assigned a priority with deadlines for action. The nature of the planning and execution can be perceived from the fact that six years after the initial confrontation meeting these results had been obtained: an expansion of research and development; marketing on a national rather than merely a regional basis; utilization of a semi-sophisticated computer

technology; a revised organization structure with a new position, Executive Vice President responsible for coordination of functions; a new line of well-received hydraulic products.

The success of the company's constructive confrontation policy was evidenced by two objective criteria: turnover among younger personnel had dropped substantially, and company sales had climbed to $8 million with before-tax profits of $1.1 million.

Case Analysis

In the story of the Old-Timers versus the Young Turks, the dissent had to do with the basic operating stance of the organization. The older, "in" group favored slow growth. The younger, less tradition-bound group wanted growth tied to a monthly rather than a yearly timetable. As is often the case in dissent, there was no right or wrong position. Thus the disagreement was particularly suited to a solution by compromise.

Without the intervention of Dr. Shapiro it's possible that the established group, which was technically in control, would have attempted a domination approach. They might have rejected the viewpoint of the Young Turks, saying in effect, "Take it or leave it." But the consequences of such a move can be destructive. The Young Turks, throttled back, would clearly have had difficulty doing their jobs. And the possibility of losing one or more key men, possibly the entire dissenting group, was a major threat to the functioning of the organization. Compromise in this case was a wise choice.

Strengths and Weaknesses of Compromise

As stated earlier, compromise may be a tempting response because it seems to be "fair" and promises to satisfy both the protester and management. After all, neither side "loses." True, neither wins, either, but most of us are so constructed psychologically that merely not losing can seem like a victory. However, despite its promise of providing an easy out, of smoothing over the questions raised by protest, compromise may bring about some unsatisfactory results. Consider the following examples:

The "half-child" decision. As one executive says, "Indiscriminate use of compromise may mean, as King Solomon threatened, that each of the parties gets half a child."

Refuge of the weak-kneed. Like partial capitulation, compromise may be used by a management that is unable to take a strong stand. In cases where a top executive cannot or will not use domination, compromise may be perceived as a "safe" recourse.

Substitute for incisive thinking. For the listening executive who doesn't want to face up to a tough decision, or who can't bring himself to do the spadework that will expose the roots and dimensions of a problem underlying the protest, compromise may seem an easy out. Complications that may arise later as a result of murky thinking now are dismissed from the mind.

Compromise also has a number of qualities that recommend it as a response:

Unity. Inherent in compromise is the possibility that it can blend two elements that are stronger in combination than either is alone. For example, an electronics company decided to shut down an assembly operation in its annex. The division manager protests the move vigorously as not being justified either by current or anticipated orders. Management's explanation is, "We can't afford to operate that unit, given its present cost efficiency." The protester says, "If we shut down and in three months want to start up again, the cost and effort will be tremendous." The final decision: operate the annex with a skeleton crew. The protester agrees that this is much better than a complete suspension, and management agrees that it now has a hedge against a sudden increase in business.

Refinement. In some cases, compromise represents an improvement on the original policy or procedure. What often happens is that the policy, as first devised, was based on the intuition and experience of the planner. The protester, with the benefit of the time-testing that the policy has undergone, can point out the deficiencies in the original. His or her suggestions for improvement can then be blended in.

The next chapter describes the response to protest called integration. It is somewhat more complex than the other four responses, but it has special virtues that recommend its use where appropriate.

CHAPTER 11

Integration—A Group Protest

Mary Parker Follett (1868–1933) was a leading business philosopher best known for her advocacy of the "integrated solution," which, like the compromise, settles conflict in a way that benefits both sides.

The integrated solution is an alternative to either-or thinking. It is also an effective alternative to compromise. It gives consideration to opposing ideas, but unlike compromise it tries to avoid a settlement that may be unsatisfactory, in part, to both parties.

A simple example serves to illustrate the elements of integration. Two employees are quarreling over whether a window near their workplace should be open or shut. One complains of a draft, the other avers that he can't breathe. A compromise solution would be to close the window half way. In that case, however, the former isn't satisfied because he still feels some draft, and the latter is dissatisfied because he is not getting as much air as he says he needs. An integrated solution would set aside the all-or-none business about the window and search for other ways to make both employees satisfied. One way to do this is to relocate the first individual in a draft-free area, and leave the second next to the open window. In short, the full objectives of both would be *integrated* into the solution.

In terms of dissent, here is how integration might come into play. At a regular top-management meeting of the Metcalf Company, the annual Christmas party is on the agenda for discussion.

Chairman Ted Groth explains, "We are more or less persuaded that we will run the same kind of affair as last year's, meaning we'll be having the party in our own recreation room again. Going outside would just push the tab too high."

There is immediate discussion. Some people agree with the decision, others make a pitch for an outside location—a nearby hotel, for example. Finally, Bill Sully says, "Ted, in my opinion there are major intangibles that should be taken into account. I think last year's affair was pretty lame. I'm for spending the money it takes to get a lively party. Frankly, I think the people here need a shot in the arm."

Sully's advocacy heats up the discussion on both sides. Finally, Groth holds up his hand for silence. "I believe there is an alternative that will satisfy all of you. What I hear you saying is that company morale would be helped by a Christmas party that is more than just a token observance. What we are after, then, is not a question of location but of spirit and liveliness. How would it be, then, if we substantially increase the budget for the affair, and set up a three-member planning committee headed by Bill Sully? Within the budget, their only consideration is to arrange the best get-together possible. If we hold the party on company premises, the additional funds will mean better entertainment and more prizes. If we have it in a hotel, we'll have to make a few adjustments, but they'll be minor."

Groth's solution is an integrated one because it sidesteps minor quibbles and gets to the heart of the matter. His solution thus has a better chance of delivering what's wanted by all concerned than do other approaches.

It may not be easy to find an integrated solution. As Mary Parker Follett herself was aware, more thought, more imagination is required to come up with an answer that transcends controversy and integrates the objectives of both parties. But in not resorting to compromise, without becoming enmeshed in partisanship, the integrated approach has obvious advantages.

The case that follows illustrates how one business conflict was handled by the response of integration.

Case of the Deferred Payday

Money matters are surefire cause for protest. Usually, the complaint is a simple matter—an accounting error, a disagreement over sick pay, and so on. The case below involved a management decision concerning all the employees; hence a sizable group banded together in submitting a petition of protest. The episode begins with an announcement from the treasurer's office of a Boston publisher.

To: All Employees
From: Bob Zora
Date: December 1

Subject: Payroll System

For many years, the payroll has been prepared through an outside firm. But now several factors, among them the company's growth and the increasing complexity of government regulations, have brought about the need for substantial improvements in the system.

After careful examination, we concluded that the most effective course of action would be to develop an internal payroll system run at our own data processing center. This system is scheduled to become effective with the first payday of next year.

The last check you will receive this year will cover the two-week period ending December 24, with distribution of that check to be on December 22. The following week, ending December 31, will be the first pay period under the new system, and will be covered by the check you receive on Thursday, January 6. Thereafter, checks will be distributed every Thursday in payment for the prior week.

Some employees immediately realized that the new procedure would likely leave people short of cash over the New Year's weekend, a time when it is often greatly needed. After considerable informal discussion, Carl Solwey, an editor, took the initiative and prepared a petition that was circulated among employees in his department. Most of them signed it and forwarded it to the office of the president. It read:

> To: Evan Greene
> From: Your employees
> Subject: The new pay period
>
> We, the undersigned, ask Management to reconsider the decision to change the pay schedule in the middle of the holiday season. This is a bad time for most people to "lose" four day's pay. It will mean particular hardship for employees in the lower pay brackets. Is there any reason why the change could not be made at, say, the end of February?
>
> Thank you.

The memo, with 30 signatures, was sent to Evan Greene, the president. Greene called in treasurer Bob Zora. Greene made it clear that he deplored the need for the petition. "We're supposed to be an enlightened management, with good employee relations," he said. "Now what can we do about this petition? Is it practical to delay the change to February?"

Actually, Greene himself realized the impracticality of changing the switchover, but he wanted his staff to appreciate his seriousness. Not surprisingly, Zora soon came back with figures to show that changing the plan would result in chaos. "We've terminated our contract with our outside computer service. It would be very costly to start it up again, or even to reprogram our own system."

Eventually, a plan was worked out that took into consideration both the fact that the change had gone too far to be reversed, and that the employees had a legitimate complaint. Any employees who suffered a hardship because of the new pay plan could apply for a short-term, interest-free loan equal to the amount of pay they would have received during the holiday period under the old system.

Case Analysis

A novel aspect of this case involves the departure from the traditional protest where an individual goes straight to his boss. Here, not only is the protest a group action, but it is directed at several levels of management. The first manager involved is treasurer Zora. The petition is not sent to him, though, but directly to the head of the company. Actually, for a group protest, this communication path is the rule rather than the exception. The head of the organization normally is the only one with sufficient authority to deal with protest from an employee group, which has a higher potential of escalating into a company-wide problem.

Although management refuses to undertake the action proposed, it does present an alternative that is essentially an integrated solution. Instead of locking horns with the employees over rights and wrongs and impracticalities, management addresses itself to the heart of the matter, namely that some people will be adversely affected by the new system. And it comes up with a practical, acceptable solution.

Employees were satisfied by management's obvious effort to neutralize the damage of the payroll procedure. Some were not altogether pleased, but even these had to admit management's concern.

In the end, management gained some real benefits from its handling of the protest. In the words of president Greene: "One thing we learned was that we had drifted into a self-deceived feeling of closeness with the employees. Communication in general had simmered down to the monthly house newsletter and an occasional message about promotions, retirements, and so on. I read into the petition a feeling of separation on the part of the employees from the company. Afterwards, I asked for a detailed review of the situation by Personnel."

Another lesson: it is desirable to get employee reactions in advance of major policy announcements where possible. Discussions about the change in the payroll setup had been entirely confined to the top echelon. At the very least, a few key supervisors, those particularly close to their employees, might have been consulted, and their sense of the employees feelings assayed. A crucial point here is that if management truly wanted such a procedure in the first place, the whole incident probably would not have occurred.

Another long-range benefit: the publishing company perceived a greater need for sensitivity to the interests and views of employees.

"We got off lightly on this one," says Personnel Director Mary George, "a low price for an important lesson."

Note that despite a few stops and starts, management succeeded in coming up with that highly desirable response to protest, the integrated solution. Note that because of it, management was able to go through with its changes as planned and that the employees—those who wanted to avail themselves of it—could apply for noninterest loans eliminating the hardship against which they were protesting, that is, a cash shortage during the Christmas season.

The management attitudes that led to the development of this response are worth noting. First, management accepted the protest in a spirit of open-mindedness, a willingness to listen.

Then, recognizing the justice of the protest, effort was made to solve the problem by reversing the decision, or at least delaying the actual change to a later date. Even though the result of the exploration was negative—that is, the results of delay would have been chaotic—management was then in a position to make another move, that is, to explore other steps that would ameliorate the difficulties.

The combination of openness and concern for the protesters' point of view, and finally, the *willingness* to make the effort to come up with a fair decision, resulted in an integrated solution in which both sides got what they wanted.

The next chapter deals with a type of protest that lies somewhat outside the framework of the five basic management responses, yet happens often enough to merit special attention.

CHAPTER 12

A Special Case—
The Unjustified Protest

AMONG the protests brought to the attention of an organization, a percentage will be unjustified. Dissenters, being human, are obviously capable of being wrong. And for reasons ranging from mild paranoia—the common garden variety to which most of us are susceptible—to misunderstanding data, complaints may be made that are not warranted.

As you would expect, the main way of dealing with this type of challenge is domination. Thus, by definition, the dissenter's views are not likely to be accepted. But because this sort of dissent poses special problems, certain steps have to be taken in order to (1) minimize disruption, (2) make the aftermath as fruitful as possible, and (3) get underneath the circumstances of the protest. The first two objectives apply to all types of protest. But it is number three that is unique to the unjustified protest and that requires special attention.

Handling unjustified protest is often especially difficult because the real motives behind the protest may be unknown even to the protester himself. The existence of this nonrational element clearly complicates the problem for the organization's representative, as the following incident illustrates.

The Les Salter Case

"Is it true that you've decided to go ahead with the pilot on this tape program?" Les Salter asks his boss, Joe Gregg, executive vice president of Universal Management Training Services.

"That's right," Gregg says. "I just cleared it with P.J. We're all set."

"I think it's a big mistake," says Salter. "We stayed out of tape programs ten years ago, when it was new. It's peaked now, and the outfits that are still marketing tape programs are extremely competitive. In my opinion, our strongest card is developing and pushing our regular services. Why go into an unfamiliar field where we'll have our head handed to us?"

Gregg listens to the division manager's statement thoughtfully. He is about to respond when Salter continues. "And one more thing. I don't believe Carl Hart has the talent to produce a tape program. It means a whole new hustle for us—hiring people, training them, diverting our energies from our regular stuff. Don't you think we ought to reconsider the decision before we work ourselves into a terrible mess?"

Gregg says, "There is a lot in what you say, Les. There are always headaches to a new undertaking, and you've hit on some major ones. But I can't give you a quick answer. Let me think about it, and come see me in the morning."

Bias or Honest Dissent?

Gregg starts thinking as soon as Salter disappears out the door. As he sees the problem, he has to work at two levels: first he has to deal with specific problems brought up by the division manager, and second, he has to address himself to Salter's feelings. Knowing him as he does, he realizes that the motive for his dissent is in large measure the rivalry between Salter and Carl Hart. Salter resents the fact that the new program is Hart's idea, and is to be produced in the latter's division. The expansion would automatically increase the scope and responsibility of Hart's job. Salter would be upstaged, and would lose ground in his race with Hart for upward movement in the organization. To Gregg, the protest is a smoke screen hiding the division manager's envy and hostility. Therefore his answer to the protester will have to take both the overt and covert aspects into account.

The next morning, when Salter comes into his office, Gregg says, "Les, as I said I would, I've rethought our decision to go ahead with the tape program. I must say that the problems you mentioned are probably real: the timing of our entry into the field may be wrong, and we're going to face some tough competition. But the fact is, the board of directors has decided that we must expand our markets if Universal is to move ahead. And the tape field, despite its difficulties, is the best bet we've been able to come up with.

"Risky? Of course," Gregg continues. "But we do have one advantage, and that is that our program is unique; it at least fills a need not touched by the competition. If we all get behind the effort—and we're counting on you to make a contribution in terms of ideas—we've got a good chance to make out. This doesn't mean we've stopped looking for expansion in other areas, or improvements in present programs. I'm hoping that you will be able to come up with some suggestions that will give us an even stronger position."

Case Analysis

Although Gregg was fairly certain that behind Salter's disagreement lay personal animosity toward Hart, the vice president chose not to address himself directly to that problem. To appreciate the wisdom in this strategy, consider the consequences if Gregg had tried to deal with the underlying causes. For example, he might have said: "Les, I understand why you're taking a dim view of the tape program. You don't like Hart, and you see this project as a scheme that may bring him sizable benefits. Why don't you just relax and see how things work out? After all, if the effort fails, you may be the guy to pick up the pieces."

This approach is undesirable for two reasons: it makes Gregg sound calculating and unprincipled, cynical to the point where the interests of the organization seem secondary; and it seems to provide an incentive for Salter to sabotage the tape program.

As a result of the vice president's wise analysis of the background situation, he decided that the best way of dealing with the protest was to minimize Hart's "victory" over Salter. He accomplished this by trying to build up Salter's self-esteem and emphasize his potential role in the new program. What Gregg did typifies an effective approach for dealing with an unjustified protest. Note the following elements of the V.P.'s method.

Receptivity. Gregg listened attentively to the protest, with no indication that he considered it invalid or merely an expression of personal animosity. In short, *he gave it the same consideration he would have accorded a justified dissent.*

Time to think. To emphasize his desire to arrive at a thoughtful solution, he postponed his response till the next day. But this was not only a ploy. On the contrary, the executive clearly felt a need to think over the situation before responding.

Management view. Gregg logically laid out the reasons behind management's decision to back the tape program. This was important in dispelling Salter's fear that he was getting a runaround.

Concession. Addressing himself to the arguments the division manager had made, Gregg didn't launch a counter argument, but went along with the things his subordinate said that made sense. Agreeing like this took the conversation out of the argument arena, and further emphasized that Salter was getting a fair hearing.

Dealing with the motivation. Finally, note that the V.P. avoided any overt mention of Salter's motives. However, suspecting what they were, he said two things aimed at lessening the division manager's dissatisfaction. He offered Salter the opportunity to become a part of the new program, and he pointed out that the door was open for activities that might increase his advantage.

Managers in Joe Gregg's position, confronted by a protest that is made not for itself but for reasons that make it essentially unjustified, will find the five elements suggested above helpful in devising a constructive approach.

In contemporary management thought there is a strong strain—based on Skinnerian psychology—which feels one should not deal with motivation but only with behavior. There is some wisdom in this approach. Where it applies most is in dealing with misbehavior or recalcitrance in the lower echelons. The problem in applying the rule indiscriminately, is that unless the motive is known, the true significance of the behavior is unclear. And this is exactly the problem with unjustified protest. Fortunately there are telltale signs that can be used to spot such a protest and reveal the motives behind it.

How to Recognize an Unjustified Protest

In the Salter case, it was accepted as a given that the protest was unjustified, and that Gregg recognized it as such because of his familiarity with the people and the situation. Knowing the protester, the issue, and the other people involved is often the key to identifying the protest spurred on by ulterior motives.

In some cases, identifying the unjustified protest is not a simple matter. The reason is that there is no hard-and-fast line between justified and unjustified dissent. An unjustified protest is invariably somewhat supportable by the "facts" and there may be a degree of emotional or covert motivation in an otherwise justified and seriously intentioned dissent. By pinning down the characteristics of unjustified protest, however, you will be able to identify not only those that are completely unwarranted, but also the unjustifiable portion in an otherwise valid protest.

Distorted presentation. A cloudy, questionable motivation is likely to show up in the things the executive says in favor of his view. "Every employee in the organization is outraged. . . ." Perhaps, but not likely. "There's not the slightest chance that management's plan can succeed." Few management decisions are ever *that* bad. The point is, look for statements that reflect more feelings than facts.

Ax-grinding. The second element of an unjustified protest is that it is a vehicle for irrelevant feelings. For example, in the Salter–Gregg case, it was the division manager's rivalry that explained his opposition. In somewhat the same way, a protest may stem from causes that have little to do with the dissent: an ego-bruising bout with a spouse, career frustrations, poor physical or mental health. It is up to the listener to use knowledge of the situation and people involved, as well as a finely tuned ear, to catch the undertones of bias.

Winston Churchill said, "We usually have two reasons for doing something: a good reason and the real reason." Experienced managers get to be experts in spotting real reasons. But it should not be inferred that because a protest is made for questionable reasons, it should be handled in a manner that makes light of the protest. On the contrary a protest should be heard and judged on its merits. If hidden motives exist, and they come into the open during a discussion, then perhaps the manager may deal directly with them. However desirable it may seem to deal with "real" reasons behind a protest, as long as they remain under the surface, the manager must proceed along lines suggested by the actual facts and opinions voiced during the presentation.

Part III deals with the ways and means of optimizing the effectiveness of dissent as a change factor in organizations. This section includes suggestions for protesters, listeners, and management itself.

PART III

Making Dissent Constructive

This section is designed to help executives and organizations develop and implement a practical and productive policy toward dissent.

The lead-off chapter reviews the ideas and procedures that are the keys to keeping dissent constructive for the dissenter. The following chapter offers guidelines for the executive whose task it is to deal with dissent and protest in the role of organization representative. Next we take up the considerations involved in the *organization's* handling of dissent. Suggestions are made to help top executives think through the pros and cons in forging productive policies. The final chapter presents the case of the "Swain Corporation," an organization in which dissent has been a respected and stimulating element from its founding.

CHAPTER 13

Facing Up to Management— With a Smile on Your Lips, Justice in Your Heart, and an Effective Technique in Your Pocket

Boss, I think we're definitely on the wrong course.
And I feel so strongly about this
I want to bring my case
before the policy committee.

THE day may roll around when you find yourself, possibly to your own surprise, cast in the role of dissenter. As has been argued all along in these pages, this represents not a setback but an opportunity. With clear thinking and a reasonable, matter-of-fact approach, you can improve the organization and add to your stature. At the very least, you can emerge from the confrontation with an enhanced reputation for clear thinking and forthrightness.

St. George and the Dragon

The need to dissent may be spontaneous—sudden awareness of the fault in a policy or a decision or of the superiority of your view. On the other hand, the decision to speak up may result from a more lengthy process in which a number of incidents lead to a climax.

However it is reached, the resolve to speak your mind creates a situation that requires not only initiative but forethought. You protest not for the sake of talking but to gain real benefits.

In this confrontation the individual, like as not, sees himself in the role of St. George, taking issue with the establishment as dragon. The thing confronted looms large and formidable. To protest effectively, you must think of yourself as pure of heart and in complimentary terms ("My idea is better") and the establishment as at fault ("How can they be so unimaginative?"). These strictures may seem to make everything look black and white. The problem with fairy tales is that they have too successfully covered over the fact that there are good dragons. If you see your organization only as "the enemy," it will handicap your communication, it may lead to self-righteousness, to impugning the standards, judgments, or motivations of the opposition, and so on when it doesn't deserve such wrath.

What follows are some suggestions on how to "pre-think" the protest, and how to enhance the effectiveness of what you say by presenting ideas or criticism in an acceptable way:

Before you say a word, clarify your feelings. There is nothing wrong with emotions on the work scene. Anger, frustration, and elation are as much at home on the job as anywhere else and, if felt, should be reflected in your communication. But intense emotions may be undesirable. First of all, it's possible to become so angry that you cannot even articulate your anger. And second, your emotions may be mixed with self-pity; thus you expose yourself to ridicule or resentment. In short, before a protest, do not eliminate, but control your emotions so that they do not distort meaning. If necessary, postpone a protest until you can regain self-control.

For example, an office manager said, "I wanted to talk to my boss in a matter-of-fact way about a disagreement I had with his attitude toward one of my subordinates, but I found myself shaking." What she felt was the tension that can build up in an individual to whom confrontation is an ordeal. The manager postponed the interview until the next day, when she was able to face up to a meeting with less nervousness.

Think through your case. Where a protest is major, where there is a good deal at stake, it pays to think through the entire situation. Questions like the following can clarify your assessment:

—Exactly what is it that I disagree with? Am I saying, "The whole company is no damn good," or am I really talking about a specific issue? "Our customer relations policy is working against us."

—Why do I disagree? Spell out the real damage or undesirability of the action or policy you want to protest. "The new customer relations policy is going to cost us some major accounts."
—What data do I have to support my contention? "I just got calls from two of our oldest and best customers expressing their resentment."
—Are there other people who think as I do? You may or may not want to seek support, but it is helpful to know whether your view is shared with others.
—What do you see as the consequences of failing to take your view into account? List the hardships, losses, damage to feelings, injured reputations, and so on.

Examine your motivation. Be clear on just what it is you seek from the confrontation. For example, if your chief objective is merely to voice resentment and you have no serious hope of getting your view accepted, it is likely that the meeting will not work out well. The limited nature of your objective may be misunderstood, and the listener is likely to wonder what all the shouting is about.

Not that there is anything wrong in simply registering disagreement. For instance it is entirely proper to say, "Walt, I want to make my feelings about that decision clear, even though I didn't say anything in the meeting. I disagree strongly with what was said. I think it was unfair and shortsighted." At the very least, however, make sure that your protest doesn't represent an act of self-assertion for its own sake, or reflect hostile feelings caused by an unrelated event.

The person whose protest comes from a desire for the heroic stance, who likes the idea of playing

St. George to the establishment's dragon, will not necessarily be discouraged even after truthfully identifying the source of his feelings. In this case, it is sometimes wise to act out your own script just to get the anger off your chest. And the fact is you are on firmest ground when, having undertaken this kind of self-examination, you know your feelings are justified.

Test your views. If you are going against a practice or policy that has broad acceptance, make sure that your stance is not the result of a misunderstanding or faulty thinking. If you have a friend or confidant, someone whose opinion you value, use him or her to help assess your case. This doesn't mean that you must be guided by your friend's opinion. But listen to the criticism. Perhaps it will clarify a misunderstanding or get you to see your ideas in a different, more reasonable light.

If the feedback you get is essentially supportive, but questions the politics of the situation—"You'd be doing yourself a lot of harm by going to the mat with the boss"—then what is required is to step back from the problem and to view it dispassionately. If you still think you are right, or that it is worthwhile to protest in any case, at least now you can proceed knowing that the chance of a misunderstanding or oversight on your part is slim. But where practical consequences of the protest are in question, consider the following.

Should You Protest?

This consideration presumably ought to be made at the very outset. It is mentioned here because, having had a chance to reflect on some of the major concepts involved, you are better able to answer the question of whether or not you should take action.

This point implies that a person may be a dissident without actually protesting. Considerations like the following may bring about the decision, not to speak up:

Timing. A major organizational event may diminish the importance or appropriateness of a protest. In a company that is struggling through a financial crisis, it may seem silly to protest about parking rules. Likewise, a dissenter on the verge of a major career change may decide it is foolish to speak up at such a late date.

Can't-win. In some cases, a protest should be made regardless of its outcome. But in others—and this is purely a subjective judgment—an individual may feel that the game isn't worth the candle, that a protest not likely to be favorably received will result in more losses than gains. To be realistic, you should consider what could happen following the unfavorable reception of a protest. A failure of any kind is, even if temporary, a setback. When the views of a dissenter have been rejected, or simply not accepted, his self-image will almost certainly be damaged. His standing in the organization may also suffer, how much depending on the nature of the protest.

A protest made tentatively, dispassionately offered only as an alternative among options, can be turned down without too much injury. However, a protest concerning a major matter on which the dissenter has totally committed himself, may create a strong identification between the person and the issue. Rejection may mean a major career setback.

Another possibility is that the protester gets stuck with unflattering labels. "John is always out there fighting for lost causes." "Suzanne is a latter-day Joan of Arc." Such labeling is not necessarily damaging. But it would be remiss of the protester, in considering his or her moves, not to think through the consequences of failure, as well as of success.

Waiting for an opportune situation. One may defer a protest in the hope that a future development may be helpful. Returning to an example used above, that of an unsatisfactory customer-relations policy, a manager who wants to take issue with it might decide to hold off until there is the first real proof of its harmfulness. With this piece of evidence, a stronger presentation can be made.

Factors on either side of the issue may wax or wane with the passage of time. A dissenter would do well to take these changes into account, and hold off making a protest until the balance is seemingly tipped favorably.

Planning the Presentation

It may be helpful to think of protesting as *persuasion,* rather than as argument, the aim being to get agreement from the listener. To do this probably requires getting the individual to change a way of looking at things. This is seldom simple. Therefore, one should expect to present a case according to a preconceived strategy designed for maximum persuasiveness.

The dissenter is out to state his or her view in its most ingratiating aspect at a meeting of some kind.

Now, some people are good at thinking on their feet: they speak easily, developing their thinking as they go along, despite pressure from the listener, the possibility of facing disapproval. But others are less effective. They have trouble thinking clearly, or expressing themselves effectively when the chips are down. And so key elements of their position may remain unsaid, forgotten in the excitement of the moment. For those whom confrontation makes especially tense, it may help to carry notes into the meeting, with key points written out.

Outlining Your Presentation

If your protest is a major one, and if you want reassurance that you are adequately prepared, an outline can help. Here is an example of how you might optimize the effectiveness of what you say:

A statement of the status quo. This is crucial at the beginning of your presentation. You want to make sure that you and the listening executive have a common understanding of the point at issue. State the established position clearly. "If I understand correctly, it's been decided that we are going to start marketing Cold Remedy X despite some unsatisfactory test results."

Reasons for dissent. Explain both the specific and general reasons why you are opposing the organization. "I'd like to tell you why I think marketing Cold Remedy X at this time is unwise." Then supply the data and other evidence that supports your stand.

"Remember what happened to the Y Company when they put their Z product on the market prematurely? Product liability suits nearly wrecked them, and it's taken years for them to recover their position with consumers. Now here are our laboratory figures. Notice how in this particular study, the experimental group fared worse than the control group. Some people say that other results cancel that one, that it is atypical. But I've checked, and it is the procedure of the most favorable studies that is in doubt. You'll find my analyses in these reports." And finally, "I want to emphasize that given the risk, it is an unwarranted move. It could ruin the company."

Your alternative. "I suggest that another study, by an outside laboratory, perhaps, would clear up the doubts."

The advantages of your alternative. "I realize that we risk financial loss in delaying, but no matter what those losses may be, they would be nothing compared to what would happen if we put an unsafe product on the market."

A specific conclusion. You may want to reassure the listener as to the purity of your motives, the strength of your convictions, and so on. This depends on the situation, and the nature of your relationship with the individual. Sum up your position in a constructive and acceptable manner. "I'm sure you agree that it is better to rethink this decision than to proceed, no matter how committed to the go-ahead some people may be."

It may be helpful if you spare the listener the burden of having to come to an immediate decision, and also if you can make a suggestion that will spread out the decision-making responsibility. "I know that even if you partially agree with what I've said, it leaves you in a tough position. Would it be possible to reconvene the committee and give me a chance to state my views to the group as a whole?"

Written or oral? For the most part, protest is best made in a meeting with the person in authority. Face to face, you can conduct a discussion in a flexible manner, taking into account information revealed by the mediator as you go along. But there are instances when a written protest is advisable. A protest representing a sizable group is likely to be best presented in the form of a letter or petition, which minimizes the confusion of feelings which all groups contain.

There are two other cases, however, where dissent may be more effective when written. One is when the dissenter may have trouble handling the emotions that revolve around the issue. The other is when it is desirable to give the executive in authority time to devise a response.

Consider the outcome. Favorable, neutral, or unfavorable, you will have to live with the results of the protest. Think about the following three key questions.

• *What would you be satisfied with?* In some cases, the best you can hope for is a modification of the thing you're protesting against—in short, a compromise. Of course, there are compromises and compromises. A modification may be little more than a gesture; or it may be a substantial compromise, one that largely satisfies the dissident. Decide in advance what sort of compromise would be acceptable, and develop a fallback position short of victory in which you spell out the minimum you will accept. In your confrontation—which is essentially a negotiation—you may want to push for this as a final stand.

• *What if you win?* It is possible that your argument may sweep the field. You may get agreement with your dissenting view. There are two points to keep in mind, in this case. The first is *implementation.* See that the favorable decision is actually carried out, encompassing the changes you have espoused. The second involves *minimizing damage.* Other people may be affected by the change—your boss, for one. It is possible that he or she may feel like a loser in a win-lose situation. Colleagues too, especially those who favored the original policy or procedure, may not be happy with the new shape of things.

You may or may not want to undertake a program of fence-mending. But it is advisable to keep disgruntled associates in mind, and not be surprised at negative reactions. In fact, be prepared to adjust your own behavior.

• *What if you lose?* Perhaps you can get another hearing, at a higher level, if you are dissatisfied with the outcome. But even if you get this opportunity, face up to the possibility that you may have to accept defeat as a result of a domination approach reasserting inarguably the superiority of the status quo.

One way to minimize the impact of being unsuccessful in a protest is to avoid exaggerating the critical nature of the action. Dissenters who suggest that they will stand or fall on the basis of the ruling, may have created a situation in which leaving the organization is necessary.

But the most reasonable attitude toward a negative ruling is a matter-of-fact manner and a calm state of mind—a well-intentioned move was made, and it failed. So what? The reaction one gets from colleagues and superiors is usually a reflection of the dissenter's own feelings. If the dissenter can live with the defeat, others certainly can.

Keeping It Constructive

A crucial requirement of dissent is that it be expressed in a manner that minimizes controversy, injured feelings, and upsets. A protest made with excessive vehemence verges on rebellion—an act of defiance, rather than an attempt to open up management to the possibility of gainful change.

Protest as PR?

It has been stated throughout that dissent has the potential of yielding benefits to the organization and to the dissident individual. To the careerist intent on making his mark in the organization, protest might be seen as an attention-getting device, a way of promoting oneself before one's peers and superiors.

On the face of it, then, you might regard dissent with a "Why not?" attitude. If protest is benign, why not use it the way a mountain climber uses rope and wedges, and climb to the higher reaches of the organization? Without dismissing the idea—yes, it's an approach that might work within reasonable limits—there are two possible drawbacks that should be considered.

The dissenter as clown. This fellow can be more amusing than helpful. When protest is used as a device for gaining objectives other than those stated in the dissent, the protester faces the hazard of becoming an organizational jack-in-the-box—too ready to pop up and too obviously on cue.

One occasionally sees this sort of behavior at meetings. Others secretly laugh at the professional protester, and after the meeting, comments run something like "You can always depend on Jack to take the contrary view" or "It will be a great day when Jack accepts the idea that other people's opinions actually have some value."

The dissenter as would-be master of intrigue. When dissent represents a political card—in other words, when it is not a sincere viewpoint but a ploy—this seldom goes by unnoticed. This becomes especially obvious when the individual mounts a series of protests.

The potential protester, then, is put in a somewhat ambiguous situation. While it is true that he may gain an advantage by the protest, especially if it brings about an improvement over the status quo, it is also true that he must behave in such a manner that the merits of the protest get the full focus of attention. His ego must be kept totally out of it. The fact that there *may* be benefits must remain in the back of the protester's mind in order for them to be forthcoming.

CHAPTER 14

How the Dragon Should Have Handled St. George

I could never divide myself from any man
upon the difference of an opinion,
or be angry with his judgment
for not agreeing with me in that,
from which perhaps within a few days
I should dissent myself.
Sir Thomas Browne

IN lodging a protest the dissenter confronts the organization, but exactly what—or who—does the protester actually confront?

Usually it is an executive of sufficient stature to speak for the organization. Often it is the dissenter's boss. As much as any other element in the dissent process, the listening executive is a key to the role that dissent plays in the organization. If the listener performs the role wisely, then the many benefits of dissent may accrue to the organization. If the listener is insincere, makes misjudgments, or fails to deal with the protester productively, then the destructive aspects of protest will prevail.

The executive who plays the role of listener has natural strengths and weaknesses stemming from his position. Symbolically one can equate the listener with the dragon in the St. George myth. Like that fearsome figure, the listening executive seems to be firmly entrenched. He usually has the power of the organization to fall back on. St. George—that is, the dissenter—seems to be woefully exposed and vulnerable by comparison.

Yet it is the very appearance of entrenched strength versus brave or foolhardy behavior that puts the organization's representative at a disadvantage. Essentially, his position is passive and defensive. The initiative lies with the dissenter. It's up to the listener to move in ways that will minimize the negative aspects of the protest and squeeze from it all possible benefits.

Though we may be taking unfair advantage of hindsight, still there seems to be little question that the poor creature St. George faced was insensitive, unrealistic, and dwelling in the past. Some latter-day counterparts may similarly fail to appraise the pluses and minuses of the confrontation in which they are seen as neither invulnerable nor invincible.

Of course, the big mistake an organization's representative may make at the outset is to see himself as a fire-breathing beast who can shrivel any challenger with a single blast. The same awareness that might have saved the dragon a dreadful end can be highly effective for the listening executive.

Concerns of the Listener

As is often the case with a seemingly impregnable position—the Maginot Line situation—the listener is not as omnipotent as appearances might suggest. Here are three situations that affect the objectivity of the listener and which he or she may find unsettling.

Mixed feelings. While it would be overstating the case to suggest that the listener is at a disadvantage vis-à-vis the dissenter, he or she is still likely to be laboring under some degree of mental stress. Like the dissenter, the listener may be of divided mind. The dissenter is playing a dual role, being on the one hand a representative of the organization, and on the other a human being with personal values.

Consequences. Just as there may be good or bad consequences for the protester, the listening executive may also have his or her actions reviewed. No one is immune from second-guessing. The way the protest is handled may demonstrate the executive's wisdom and sure hand in dealing with people, or it could backfire and cause grave repercussions. The executive may in turn have to face the ordeal of being judged.

Bypassing. An immediate worry of the executive is the threat that if the protester is not satisfied with the response, he or she may take the complaint to an individual of higher status. This person, in turn, would be in a position to judge not only the worth of the protest but the behavior of the first listener as reported by the protester.

This is not to say that the upper-echelon executive would necessarily believe the protester. But, as far as the first listening executive is concerned, the possibility now exists that he or she will be asked to appear before the higher executive and explain the stance. The transition from judge to material witness or even defendant should be enough of a threat to ensure that the first executive give the dissenter a fair hearing.

Protest Amid Instability

The view that has been given of confrontation so far has assumed a fairly tranquil environment. The two principals have been secure in jobs which exist in a stable and unruffled atmosphere. But in reality, the situation may be quite different. For example, in an organization in which there exists a sense of hostility and strife, a protest may represent just one more irritant—another source of upset. There may be a struggle between factions that bears on the protest in one way or another.

In such an environment, deliberation is essential. An emotional employee, burning with a feeling of injustice, may find it impossible to be calm or coherent. But if his emotions are not buffered by a stable work environment, his protests will only add fuel to the fire. His fight will be in vain. Similarly an angry or upset boss listening to a protest may soon change what started out to be a rational process into a vituperative exchange.

House Politics

Another background factor that may further complicate the boss's role is the possibility that "house politics" is putting him under a lot of pressure. For example, Henrietta Smith is remonstrating with her boss: "Mr. Kirk, we're going to have to ease up on the work schedules. We're under such pressure that I haven't had a full lunch hour any day this week. Everybody else seems to be in the same situation."

Ordinarily this would be a simple matter, judged on the basis of the facts. Kirk could verify Smith's claim and take some kind of action. But it's not so simple in this case. Kirk does not have a free hand. His boss has sent down the word: "Kirk, your department seems to be falling behind. I hear from Bill Gench that he was held up for half a day last week because the orders were jammed up in your department."

Now, the name of Bill Gench was mentioned by chance. Kirk happens to be in competition with Gench for a promotion and this becomes a factor not only in what Kirk is told, but his reaction to it. The screws are tightening, and his reception of Henrietta Smith's protest is influenced by that fact. The point, here, is that the listener, for a number of reasons, may be far from objective. Not only may he have personal biases and values, but organizational or career interests can come into play.

Organization vs. Personal Values

The organization's representative is not necessarily an impartial judge. But for him, at least, the most serious problem arises when there is a conflict between what he is supposed to feel as an agent of the organization and what he really feels as a result of personal attitudes and values. When these clash, the individual undergoes major stress.

In the ordinary course of business life, executives are supposed to unify personal and organizational attitudes. "The thing that makes managers most effective is their complete identification with organization goals." Or so stated one executive at a management seminar, to the applause of the top brass present. It is probably even true that the higher up the ladder a manager goes, the more his personal values coincide with organization goals. But the expectation that managers will identify completely with their organizations seems more nostalgic than practical, a harking back to the days of the gray flannel suit and corporate conformity.

Today, executives' feelings about what makes life—and work—worthwhile appear to be changing from those of managers of earlier generations. Nevertheless, when it becomes apparent that the interests of the organization do not coincide with your own, it can be deeply disturbing. And it is often in the executive's role as arbiter of protest that the divergence of personal and organizational views are apt to emerge. For example, note the difficult situation of executive Lee Gould.

Gould is saying to Larry Kincaid, "That's the way it is, Larry. The word from the front office is that several people on the staff are going to have to be let go. You know how I feel about this. I've always felt we were good friends. . . ."

Kincaid replies, "I'm just not going to take this lying down, Lee, not after 22 years with this company and working my ass off to do a top-notch job. You're just going to have to go back in there and make a pitch for me."

Gould shakes his head. "I'm sorry, Larry, I really am, but what you're asking just isn't in the cards. You know how bad business has been."

"I've heard that story before. As long as the company survives I expect to be on the payroll. I've earned that right."

Gould looks at the other man quietly for a moment and then says, "You're really making it tough for me. Can't you imagine how I feel, having to fire the best friend I have in this organization? But there's nothing else I can do. Don't you think I've already been up to the office, trying to get them to change the signals? I got back only five minutes ago after a second try. It's just no dice, Larry."

Even in the depths of his ordeal, Kincaid looks at Gould and realizes the hopelessness of his position. He's out, and that's the way the cookie crumbles.

What Price Objectivity?

The conflict between an individual's personal values and organizational responsibilities can be a serious problem for employees at any level. As is clear in the case of Lee Gould, responding to a friend's protest may make it impossible to carry out what to the company is a reasonable policy. Attempting to function as both friend and company executive, the difficulty in being objective is underscored.

In short, the boss who listens to an employee's protest might not be able to render even-handed justice—which is exactly what is required. The dissenter, in undertaking a protest, does so on the assumption of a fair hearing, with the case judged on its merits. But how is the listener to neutralize the pressures and influences that may sway not only his judgment but color the way he actually hears the complainant's speech? Despite the possibility of divided feelings, the executive in authority must behave in a way that satisfies his sense of integrity, and also gains for the organization any possible benefits of protest. There are three things the executive should try to ensure:

1. *A fair hearing.* Not only must the dissenter be tolerated and listened to in a passive sense, but positive action must be taken to ensure a feeling of fairness and interest.
2. *A reasonable judgment.* The response to the protest should be defensible and rational.
3. *Constructive aftermath.* The results should be helpful to the dissenter, the listening executive, and the organization.

Having accepted these goals, it is incumbent upon the executive to watch out for the following. When dealing with a protest, don't regard it as just one more personnel problem. Any presentation that comes under the heading of protest deserves special attention; after all, some of the cases may be crucial to the future of the organization. The nature of the issue may make it advisable too.

Prepare. If the seriousness and complexity of the issue warrants, familiarize yourself with the background of the situation prior to the meeting. There are facts to verify, data to collect, views of various individuals to ascertain.

In matters dealing with some staff function—the business office, Personnel, and so on—you may want to confer with executives or experts to learn what you need to know to discuss the issue with the dissenter.

Preparation actually presupposes a prior knowledge of the subject of the protest. If you haven't had enough advance notice, suggest that the protest be resumed at a later date, if only a few hours later. Issues that concern the entire organization might be discussed with your superior, so that any questions of company policy or views can be clarified. This precaution helps you to avoid making a statement or judgment that just has to be taken back later on.

Be open, but don't overfacilitate. Good communication requires that people have access to you, and that they be assured of a satisfactory meeting. To further help put the dissenter at ease, the meeting should be free of interruption and should be sufficiently private to encourage unencumbered conversation.

These, of course, are merely the ABC's of good management practice. But protest is a special sort of confrontation. It is important to shun some of the usual amenities of business conversations. Don't make the dissenter feel too relaxed, too much at ease. This would subvert the purpose of the meeting, for the aim is not to seek good rapport, but to give consideration to an employee who, more emotional than usual, wants to protest against some aspect of organizational life or practice. Watering down this serious matter with pleasantries and good fellowship would be pointless.

Mitigating steps may be taken if the dissenter has trouble setting forth the protest. For example, you should try to relieve an employee of feeling threatened or guilty. It may not be easy for him to oppose the establishment. Where this is the case, you might say something like, "Every organization can benefit from differences of opinion. I personally feel that opposing views can produce important new ideas."

Be aware of the various pressures on you. When dealing with a dissenter, you may be experiencing a number of conflicting feelings. Your loyalty to the organization may be threatened. You may feel that the employee—probably your subordinate—is being disloyal to both the organization and you. You may find a clash between your personal views on the subject and those of the organization. The fact that some of these protective or defensive feelings seem unwarranted may not be enough to stop having them. But knowing that you might have to struggle to be objective can help you become more so.

Assess motivation. During the hearing, and in considering your decision, give some thought to the purpose behind the protest. Admittedly, there is one school of management thought that avers that one must deal with behavior, not motivation. But as was pointed out in Chapter 12, there are some acts—and protest is one of them—in which it is almost impossible to deal with the behavior if you cannot identify motivation. Even in cases where protest is a screen for hostility, they should still be dealt with on their merits. But if the management representative is able to pinpoint underlying purposes, he would do well to take these into account in making a judgment.

The protester who is primarily interested in an act of self-assertion, or even in simply harassing the management representative for some personal reason, must also be heard out. But then, it will be of considerable help if the listening executive, in identifying the real reasons for the protest, takes measures that will effect a long-range remedy.

Help spell out the message. You should be listening attentively to what's said, but in some cases the individual may be under so much tension that he has difficulty expressing himself clearly. If so, do what you can to put him at ease, and, if necessary, help clear things up for him. For example, you might need to sum up the person's arguments. "What you're saying then, Phil, is that you think cutting the budget on that project represents a no-confidence vote on your idea?"

Clarify areas of misunderstanding. Early in the conversation you may discover that all or part of the protest was made because of a misunderstanding. If so, clear things up immediately. "You're mistaken about that, Henry. No one has made any commitment on that matter. It is still in the discussion stage. Anything you've heard to the contrary is not true."

Explain the rationale behind the establishment's position. In some cases misunderstanding may result from an incomplete knowledge of a particular situation. Most often this is the result of a subordinate not understanding the reasons behind a particular decision or move. "We're opening a plant in Dallas, not because we're dissatisfied with operations here, but because gradual market changes require that new location."

Compare the dissenter's view with that of the organization. It is often highly useful for both you and the protester to factually compare his case with the establishment's. Your neutrality, however, is essential. Any tendency to weight the comparison against the dissenter turns the discussion into an argument, and once this takes place it becomes difficult for the dissenter to be calm and for you to be objective.

Reach a definite conclusion. Some well-intentioned organizations and executives feel that the main purpose of hearing a protest is to give the dissenter the chance to speak his mind. This kind of reception—that is, a willingness to listen but a disinclination to take any real measures—may hush the employee temporarily, but eventually he begins to feel that he has just been manipulated.

In making your judgment, keep in mind the five options described in Part II, the possible responses to protest: domination, containment, capitulation, compromise, and integration.

Here are some of the possible conclusions of this type of conversation. Note that some are temporary and these must be followed by more definite outcomes:

- Need time to evaluate.
- Dissenter is partially correct and his or her views will be used to modify present practice.

- The dissenter is wrong for the following reasons. . . .
- Dissenter is correct and changes will be made.

Hearing in a Higher Court?

Some issues may not be settled by you or anyone else at your level. A protest that involves basic policy may require the attention of the highest echelons of management. If for any reason you decide that the issue should be dealt with up the line, you must then act as the liaison between the dissenter and the upper-level executives, so that the matter can proceed to a conclusion.

But there is another situation that may require attention from people in the upper echelons: when the protester refuses to accept the judgment given in the first hearing. The employee may be so enamored with his idea that a refusal is not acceptable. And unless the situation clearly does not call for another hearing—as when the issue is totally absurd—it's desirable to facilitate the subsequent hearing.

Pushing for the Benefits

It is a basic thesis of this book that protest holds benefits for all parties involved. These may or may not accrue automatically. Even where they do, there may be minor details that require attention. But where the benefits do not flow naturally, it is up to the executive in authority to see to it that they are forthcoming. The checklist below suggests some useful procedures.

If the judgment is favorable—

- Upper-echelon individuals involved must be briefed.
- All steps must be taken to make sure that the change actually takes place. For example, a new plan or procedure must now be implemented.
- Announcements, where relevant, should be made. These may range from a "To All Employees" memo to a briefing with key groups.
- Praise, credit, reward—recognition—should be given the dissenter for his or her efforts. (This signals, by implication, the desirable and constructive role of dissent in the organization.)
- Those who may have been negatively affected should be informed, and inconveniences or hardships minimized.

If the judgment is unfavorable—

- Ease the blow for the dissenter. The turnoff, at worst, should be temporary. If appropriate, give him public recognition for the effort.
- Reconsider the protest to see if at least some aspect of it is meritorious. You may want to ask the dissenter himself to help with this reexamination.
- Show your appreciation loudly and clearly. "Make no mistake about it, Pat. I appreciate and admire your willingness to stick your neck out on a matter of principle. Even though the decision didn't go your way, please under-

stand that we are always interested in the best efforts of everyone, no matter what happens in the end.

The Organizational View of Dissent

Does your organization actually have a policy toward dissent? Is this policy—limited, perhaps, to an attitude or tradition—generally adhered to in day-to-day practice? The next chapter can be of help to those who are unsure of how to answer these key questions.

CHAPTER 15

Organization Policy—Making Dissent Respectable and Productive

Dissent is constructive, healthy,
and an essential ingredient in the continuing
decision-making process of an organization.
It is not a four-letter word.*

AN organization may be kindly disposed toward dissent, and want to seek its benefits. But there is a common problem that may have to be acknowledged and coped with before the organization can reap any advantages.

* Statement of a top executive of the "Swain Corporation." See Chapter 16.

The fact is, dissent is most productive when the organization takes cognizance of it and adopts policies that promote the process. But this must not be taken to mean that dissent is to be encouraged, in the sense that it becomes an approved, smiled-upon function. This approach would pervert the nature and usefulness of disagreement.

Dissent, as the dictionary points out, is a "nonconcurrence with a decision of a majority," and "a difference of opinion." The values and ideas represented by dissent hold potential benefits for management in the very fact that they are in opposition to the prevailing view.

Dissent has value because it poses an alternative to the establishment way. To institutionalize it to the point where it is invited would destroy its cutting edge. Dissent improves matters through the heat that results from intelligent people opposing one another. Management, then, must be careful not to weaken with overacceptance the counterthrust to the status quo that dissent represents.

Forging a Policy

Designing a policy that nurtures dissent is not simple. In ordinary situations, say, when management wants to boost output, the options available are easily identified: add capacity, improve equipment, further train the employees, and so on. But the rewards of dissent cannot be gained by such direct or quantifiable measures. Urging people to dissent is useless—at the very least the enriching hybridization is less likely to take place. A policy and procedure that seeks to foster dissent cannot, therefore, be developed naively. An effective policy must encompass the dilemma: what you want you can't ask for. If there is any "asking" at all, it is by indirection, by creating a facilitating climate.

When incorporated into organizational life at the policy-making level, the following elements can help along the dissent process.

Building receptivity. There are few organizations in which policies on handling dissent are put in writing, and yet every organization reflects in its attitudes and traditions unique ways of viewing dissent. In addition to the "organization way," the feelings of individual officials is a major factor. A generally enlightened organization may have authoritarian executives who try to discourage protest. Similarly, relatively authoritarian organizations may have enlightened executives who go out of their way to treat dissenters constructively.

Notwithstanding the variations that result from individual executives' attitudes, every organization should have, if not a policy, at least a general awareness of dissent and the need for guidance on the part of those who must deal with it. A favorable attitude at the top induces similar feelings in the lower echelons. Positive and negative reinforcement—praise for dissent well handled, criticism for that mishandled—further establishes management's commitment to the process of dissent.

The psychic benefits of dissent. Interviews with managers who chafe at dissent, who resent it as an intrusion on management's prerogatives, usually reveal some ignorance of its indirect benefits.

Peter Drucker has pointed out that to employees

at all levels "the problem of dignity and fulfillment—of status and function—is real. . . . The problem cannot be solved alone by more or better opportunities for advancement or greater economic rewards."* The human need that Drucker describes is at least partially satisfied by dissent, which is essentially an act of self-assertion, a statement of individuality. It is for this reason that the act of dissent should be received favorably even if the substance of the protest is rejected. What managers must learn to appreciate is that dissent reinforces the integrity and freedom of the employee.

Compensate for inexperience. The danger in over-encouraging protest has already been mentioned. Yet it can be helpful, particularly for the inexperienced manager and for those whose personalities make dealing with disagreement difficult, to outline criteria for a productive and systematic approach. Most mature managers know what to do. But in instances where individual managers have difficulty grasping the spirit and practice of your policy, the rudiments of an acceptable procedure should be taught, perhaps using a handbook put out by Personnel.

Blend with the organization's communications system. It is undesirable to handle dissent as though it were taking place in a vacuum. Dealing with dissent should involve all the usual communications pathways. Every organization has its own patterns of communication: weekly management meetings, periodic reports to employees, special councils of

* Peter Drucker, *The Concept of the Corporation,* New York, The John Day Company, 1972.

managers and subordinates, junior boards of directors, and so on. The work-a-day world of management should not deviate much in the face of dissent. The presentation of and response to protest should receive a fair amount of exposure so that everybody directly involved or merely interested can know what happened.

Remember the hazards. For management, two potentially difficult situations may be triggered by dissent. The first involves legal repercussions, the other a snowballing of employee hostility. *The Wall Street Journal* reported the case of an auto company supervisor who was coming along well in his career, having started as an assembly-line worker, and rising to a management-level job in testing and product development. Unexpectedly, his department was eliminated, and the manager, Richard M., then 53 years old, was demoted to a position of engineer.

Indignant and upset, and feeling that he wasn't getting any satisfaction from his immediate superiors, Richard M. fired off a letter to the chairman of the company. Eventually he got a call from the personnel department saying his claims of unfairness weren't valid. He then decided to sue for reinstatement to his former position.

In court, the company argued that Richard M. was demoted without having to take a cut in pay at a time when "thousands of employees were being released outright" due to a recession. Richard M. countered that in his department there was actually a 15 percent net gain in personnel during that same period. And, although his salary wasn't cut (he was earning about $45,000), he says he "lost prestige, a private office, a secretary, and any right to a bonus."

He declared, "I didn't have any illusions that I could go much higher than one more notch, but the demotion put me further back in the pack for any future advancement."

The Wall Street Journal describes the Richard M. case as one of an increasing number in which middle managers go to court over what they feel is unfair treatment. Discrimination on the basis of age is common among these suits. Federal law prohibits discrimination based on race, religion, or national origin, and any time these factors underlie a protest, there is the possibility of a suit. Of course, discrimination is not the only thing that leads to legal action. For instance, suits are frequently filed for breach of an employment contract.

The "snowball" situation can be exceedingly hard to handle. Usually the protest begins with an individual's complaint. If he is treated particularly unfairly, others may rally around him. The organization is then confronted with a situation of larger and more serious dimension. This usually happens one of two ways. First, a protester's peers may side with him, even though they have no direct interest in the organization's capitulating to the dissident. Nevertheless, perhaps because of his leadership qualities or his popularity, others line up behind him.

Second, the dissent may focus on an issue of direct interest to all employees. For an example of this development see "Case of the Deferred Payday" in Chapter 11. Whenever a large number of employees stand to benefit personally from one person's supplication, you can bet that many will go to bat for him. Group protest, with its threat of serious divisiveness, confronts management with a problem that goes beyond the scope of this book. All that can be said is that the best way to minimize the problem, if not eliminate it, is to treat protesting employees fairly. And management should train its representatives to recognize the possibilities of legal action or group protest, and to learn how to contain such dissent at an early stage.

Tailor the policy. There is one cardinal quality your policy must have: it must be of a piece with the climate of your organization, particularly in its degree of authoritarianism. There should be congruence between the organization's character and its philosophy concerning protest.

For example, Company A is a small organization with a tightly-knit group of top people who share a vision and strategy for achieving its objectives. This company, with its strong central authority, is unproductive soil for contrary views. Rather than try to graft on to the organization a policy toward dissent that is out of character with its basic outlook, it would be more appropriate to openly discourage dissent. This does not mean total repression, but that disagreement should be kept within well-defined limits. There is no pretense that management "is always interested in hearing what people really think."

Company B, on the other hand, is idea hungry, and relishes the heat that can be created in rubbing two opposing ideas together. It welcomes dissent, doing almost everything but put up posters to get its managers to speak their minds. In such a company it would be foolish, even damaging, to adopt a conservative policy toward dissent.

One last point: a policy should also reflect what managers down the line will not only accept but support.

Review and assessment. Dissent is the sort of activity that goes on virtually constantly, and yet large numbers of executives are unaware of it because it doesn't touch them personally. The average top executive would understandably have difficulty answering questions like the following:

- How would you rate your organization in terms of how effectively it handles dissent?
- Is dissent a lively, active process?
- Too lively?
- Do your managers think dissent yields benefits?
- Do they know what the benefits are?
- Do they know how to make sure that these gains are actually derived?
- Do the managers know *your* attitude toward protest?
- Do your managers themselves dissent from time to time?
- If not, why not?

If you find your answers to be rather negative or vague, it is likely that you have come upon a top-priority agenda item for the next few management meetings. How far top executives should go in briefing managers on the benefits from dissent will vary from individual to individual. But in cases where a review suggests that conformity is devitalizing the organization, clearing the way for lively intelligent dissent is an obvious antidote.

CHAPTER 16

Getting It All Together—One Company's Approach

EARLY in the research for this work, the author spent some time with a New England firm that has a reputation for its effective approach in handling dissent. The purpose was to see firsthand what can be achieved in an organization in which dissent is regarded favorably. In brief, the company is a medium-size manufacturer of a broad range of consumer goods, dealing in plastics and allied materials. It is a near-autonomous division of a 75-year-old parent firm which operates internationally. All names, including that of the firm, are pseudonyms.

Why Does Swain Love Dissent?

Appropriately enough, Swain Corporation was formed as a result of dissent. Its founder and present president, Bill Swain, disagreed with peers in the parent company over the makeup of its product list. He had become interested in plastics in 1950 and wanted the company to set up a new plastics division. Top management rejected the idea. Swain then went out on his own and was able to find sufficient financial support to start up the plastics operation. The enterprise prospered and eventually he reunited with the parent company—the word "parent" can be taken almost literally, since it is a family-run organization.

It is quite probable that Swain's personal experience was a cornerstone of the Swain Corporation's dissent policy. The president obviously had good reason to recognize the value of a minority opinion. And his personal style in management meetings sounds a keynote for dissent: he routinely asks his managers what's wrong with his ideas, and he listens to what they say. His willingness to entertain differing opinions, and to yield to them when they are persuasive, sets a pattern that persists down the line.

Organization Policy

Swain Plastics has nothing in writing on how executive dissent should be handled (although like most other organizations it has a written "Employee Complaint Procedure" for lower-echelon employees). But Swain nevertheless asserts that it has a philosophy toward dissent: it sees "professional disagreement as a healthy, essential ingredient in the continual decision-making process of an organization." As Greg Gaynes, vice president in charge of Production, puts it, "We know that dissent is not a four-letter word."

From Philosophy to Practice

Based on its avowed policy, Swain has developed a procedure to handle executive dissent. When there is disagreement from a professional about a management decision, goal, or policy, a face-to-face confrontation between the principals is arranged. The executive has the opportunity to present his case while the management representative listens. The two discuss the matter until some kind of mutual understanding is reached. Unresolved matters go to the next higher authority, and eventually to Bill Swain, if need be. Sometimes these confrontations occur spontaneously at a meeting. If practical, the discussion is held then and there. If not, a follow-up meeting is arranged between the people directly involved.

To a large extent it is felt that the success of dissent depends on how skillfully the executives play the role of dissenter. Tradition suggests the following guidelines.

Timing. Swain executives say that timing often depends on house politics. Dissent which ignores tempers and pressures of the moment is likely to be ignored itself. Peripheral issues may have to wait indefinitely for the rush of urgent business. Also, protest that is belated will not get sympathetic hearing at Swain. Says Gaynes, "We can't realistically deal with protest against a new program that's already well under way." However, dissent aimed at central matters will always get full attention.

The dissenter's approach. Paul Harris, vice president of Personnel, points to two middle managers who have frequently spoken out against executive policy at staff meetings as examples of the right and wrong way to dissent. The effective manager uses a "professional," tactful manner, saying in effect, "You may be right, but I disagree." He then brings out flow charts, reports, and statistics to support his opinion. The ineffective manager starts out with, "You're all wrong!" and attacks the personalities and integrity of the people present, rather than deal with the issue at stake. When the dust has settled this dissenter has hacked away at the reputations of his peers and insulted various individuals. Says Harris, "Even if he's on the right side of the question, he is usually ignored because of the manner in which he handled the situation. This may not exactly be justice but it is the hard reality of interpersonal relations."

Both men gain visibility from their acts of dissent, but the first is respected for his ideas and approach, while the second man's views are killed off by his own offensive style.

Henry Bell, a middle manager, adds another dimension to the matter of the dissenter's approach: "When I disagree with my boss or some aspect of company policy, how I go about it depends on the person I'm confronting. What I say, how I say it, and perhaps even *if* I say it, depends on who I'm talking to. I know I can be open with my boss. Frankly, I'm less trustful with other people.

"After years of watching, listening, and getting to know the top people in Swain I now feel I know how to approach each one in a way that is most effective in getting my point across. I seldom hold back anything because I don't feel that I have to in this company. But it makes good sense to keep in mind the personalities involved when I'm about to rock the boat."

Hard data. At Swain, the dissenter's status may be a factor. "I'm talking practice, not theory," admits Gaynes. He explains, "A manager voicing dissent in the upper echelons had better have logical, sound reasons to substantiate his views. A top executive can propose or oppose action for emotional reasons and even win out because of his status. But this happens very rarely."

Bill Swain himself has wanted to build a production plant on the West Coast for a number of years. He has a strong hunch in favor of the expansion, feeling that this sort of growth would be very good for the organization. But every time he brings up the subject, a manager two levels below disagrees, showing the boss why it isn't feasible to build such a plant. His opinion is backed by figures and projections of various kinds. As the president of the company, Swain could order that the plant be built. Yet, he respects the manager's reasoned view. Result: no plant—as yet.

Honor for the Dissenter

Swain respects the fact that the manager is doing what he is being *paid* to do, to use his knowledge and experience in guiding the organization in what he considers to be the right direction, regardless of established management views or opinions. Contrary opinions cut across all echelons. Gaynes, Swain's second in command, has wanted to add another product line to one area of the business. But a small group of his subordinates has successfully opposed this effort, armed as it was with hard facts to the contrary.

Bill Swain confesses to a personal way of dealing with dissent from a lower echelon. Instead of trying to crush it with his authority, he tries to "politick" these subordinates individually, hoping that his personal persuasiveness might get them to change their minds. But being unsuccessful in these efforts, he goes along with their objections. As he says, "If these people were yes-men we would now have a production plant on the West Coast, a whole new product line—and a variety of headaches with both."

A Cost Accounting Supervisor Speaks Up

Swain Plastics' cost accounting supervisor regularly attends product-pricing meetings. He has no hesitation in telling Swain or any other executive in the company that he doesn't agree with their determination of selling prices. He realizes that they must make the final decision but feels strongly that it's *his job* to make them understand the cost accounting aspect of the issue, on which he's an expert. He doesn't see his dissent as a negative factor, but as a positive contribution necessary to the decision-making process. "They're paying for a lot of years of professional experience," he says. "It's my job to give my opinion whether they want to hear it or not. And I believe that they listen to what I'm saying. We may not agree, and as a matter of fact, I'm usually the voice of dissension in the room. But as they invite me to all the meetings, I assume that they want my opinion."

Persistence—As a Matter of Course

Harris of Personnel describes a case in which the head of one of the divisions responded to the dissent of a subordinate by saying, "You're out of your mind!" "But," says Harris, "since the subordinate felt strongly about his idea even after the rejection, he returned to his office, restudied the situation, and built a case for his position. He then returned to his boss, attempting again to convince him of the value of his alternative procedure.

"Aware of the company tradition toward disagreement, the executive felt he had to give the subordinate another hearing. Consequently, he listened more objectively the second time around. He assimilated the facts and figures and, perhaps reluctantly, agreed to the superiority of the subordinate's ideas." Harris summed up his feelings about dissent as follows: "At Swain, a subordinate who is intimidated by the first put-down, who hesitates to contradict or offer contrary opinions, hasn't learned very much about the company and the way it's run and usually doesn't stay here very long."

Right Now vs. Later

Executive Gaynes points out the need to balance disagreement at once against holding off until a more convenient time. "There are two minor problems with immediate confrontation. One is that it may become overly emotional, and the other is that an impromptu confrontation may disrupt people's work schedules.

"Both problems are minor, though," Gaynes continues, "compared to those that might arise when a confrontation is put off for even a few days. We find it's better for the company and for the people involved to get the difficulty out into the open. Let people vent their anger and frustration and get the problem resolved. 'Justice delayed is justice denied' is as true here as in a court of law. And from an operating standpoint it makes sense to quickly remove doubt and disagreement, which can become serious obstacles to smooth operation."

Refinement of Ideas

Swain executives say that dissent represents a good system of checks and balances. Any decision or policy which is shaky or ineffective will be questioned sooner or later. And because of the spirit of openness the dissent usually is voiced in time to prevent serious consequences.

One executive says that when a decision of his is questioned by a subordinate he stops to think the decision through from the other person's perspective. As a result he's either more sure of his original decision or is able to make it stronger based on the suggestions of the dissenting subordinate.

A Bawling Out—but with Heart

From Gaynes's files comes a memo written to a dissenting subordinate that points up two of the important aspects of dissent at Swain. One is the complete acceptance of the individual's right to dissent. The other is the company representative's policy of playing it completely straight with the dissenter. Not surprisingly, there is no coddling in the memo. The friendly and direct tone of the communication speaks for itself. Overall, the approach is an interesting example of a domination response used with warmth and understanding.

Dear Bob,

You're wrong on this one—and isn't that a helluva way to start a dialog?

Of course, I'm counting on our friendship, our mutual respect, and your magnanimity to offset my disagreement with you.

You have a most refreshing and original spirit which this company can use well, and your vitality, your action-oriented drive, your ability—all properly channeled—will make a tremendous and healthy contribution to the continued growth of our company. Yet I can't buy your view that you're being done badly by. It is not my intention to "take a lot away from your office. . . ." I would like to see your office grow within our company. But this can only be done when you begin to realize fully how important it is for you to learn from those around you and get them to want to see your position expand.

So, Bob, do your thing—insist that each man do his job. Help him do that job, let him take the credit and recognition. You must give others their own identity, and build up those around you. And you must temper your eagerness to make a quick track record. When you share the limelight which you personally enjoy so much, the "mistreatment" you are protesting will not again come into question.

Training for Dissent

Paul Harris, head of Personnel, describes the orientation managers are given: "Our new managers go through a six-week general training program. During this time they receive some guidance on how to handle dissent from their subordinates and also on how to express their *own* dissent to *their* supervisors. We get across our philosophy that dissent is healthy for the company if presented constructively, that it is stimulating and educational, and should be nonthreatening for the people involved. And we stress that we expect it and accept it at all levels."

Harris adds, "When we bring in or promote someone to a management position we know pretty well beforehand—through psychological testing and personnel interviews—how that manager's style will fit in with our corporate personality. That's a major reason we don't usually have to spend a lot of time explaining our concept of 'creative dissent.' We already know that his philosophy is not opposed to that of the company."

Why the Policy Works

Harris explains why the company has maintained its favorable attitude toward protest despite occasional upsets and operational delays: "We feel we've derived great advantages from our philosophy toward dissent. And we feel the concept works for us because of the sense of job security our people have here at Swain. An employee who thinks he or she is going to be fired for an arbitrary, frivolous, or emotional reason will never have the courage to express a controversial opinion. We have tried to build up an attitude of trust so that people can feel comfortable expressing their dissent.

"This is a benefit we all derive. We're aware that our approach won't work in every company. There are even some organizations that may run better without dissent, where one person calls the shots and managers just follow orders. But if an organization feels it can benefit from original thinking and the trading of ideas, then I think our method of handling disagreement—of channeling that energy into something positive—works well and I recommend it strongly to other organizations."

Bill Swain has the final word. "I don't want to sound off in some simplistic, fatuous way, but I do feel that entertaining disagreement is a natural extension of democracy. I think that in our system dissent and protest have a natural place. The freedom to disagree along with the privilege of being heard is one of the great virtues of our way of doing things."

Index

A

B

C

D

E

F

G

H

I

J

L

M

N

O

P

Q

R

S

T

U

V

W

Y